North
Hill.

ALICE ELGAR

Enigma of a Victorian Lady

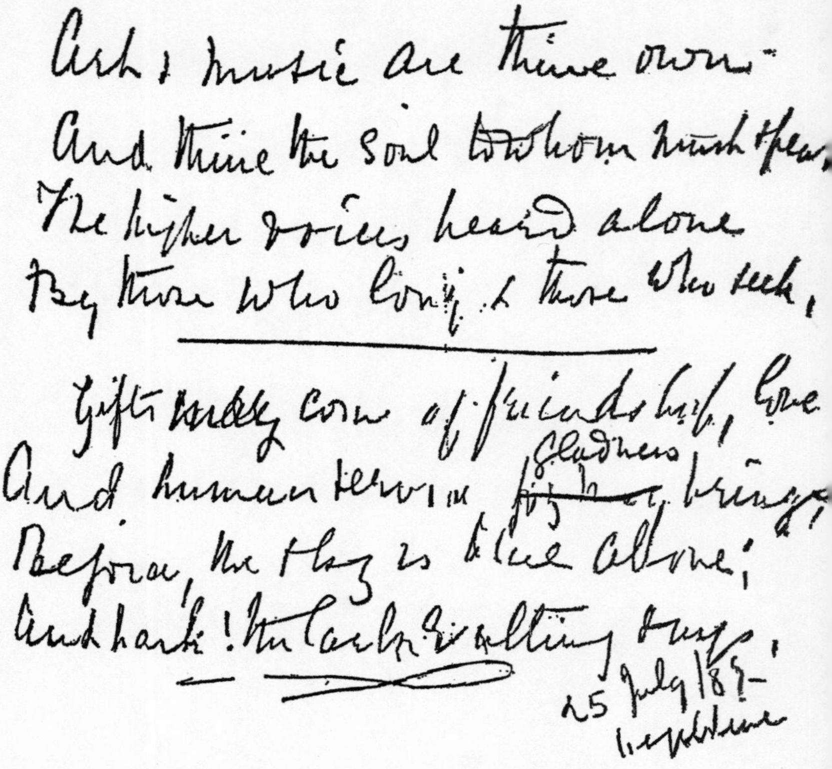
Art & music are thine own —
And thine the soul to whom much speak,
The higher voices heard alone
By those who long & those who seek,

Gifts today come of friendship, love
And human sorrow gladness brings;
Before, the sky is blue above;
And hark! the lark's exulting songs.

25 July 87 —
Hazeldine

"Art and Music . . ." by Alice Roberts, Hazeldine, 25 July 1887

ALICE ELGAR

Enigma of a Victorian Lady

Percy M. Young

London
DENNIS DOBSON

First published in Great Britain in 1978 by Dobson Books Ltd,
80 Kensington Church Street, London W8 4BZ.

ISBN 0 234 77482 7

Printed in Great Britain by
Clarke, Doble & Brendon Ltd, Plymouth and London

Acknowledgements

For assistance on various points of detail I am indebted to: Mr. Wilfrid Blunt, Curator of the Watts Gallery, Compton, near Guildford; Rev. R. Burleigh, formerly Rector of Redmarley d'Abitot; Rev. E. M. Fortune, Vicar of Berrow; Dr. T. A. Heathcote, Curator of The Sandhurst Collection, Royal Military Academy, Sandhurst; Mrs. Jutta Dougan; Mrs. Gladys M. Reed; Mrs. Pauline Rohatri, of the India Office Library in the Foreign and Commonwealth Office; Miss Rouse; the Librarians of the *Daily Telegraph*, Gloucester City Library, Gwent County Library; and the County Archivist, Shire Hall, Gloucester.

The portrait of Major-General Roberts and painting of The Battle of Banas are reproduced by permission of the India Office Library and Records; the photographs of Redmarley *c.* 1890 were kindly made available by Miss Rouse of Redmarley. Renée Morris Young has taken some of the pictures included in this book, to whose author she has given support in innumerable ways.

P.M.Y.

Contents

Illustrations

Introduction

Within the conventions obtaining at the present time it may be said that within every wife there is a woman waiting to break out. Since female liberation is a *Leitmotiv* of our age it is proper to cast back over some of the by-passed tributaries of history to discover where and to whom reparation is due. A principal candidate, by any reckoning, is Caroline Alice Roberts, hitherto summarily dismissed as "Lady Elgar".

To be the wife, or the mistress, of a creative artist in whatever field is a hazardous occupation. Contrary to popular belief this is not because male artists are morally inferior, or mentally less stable, than other men; it is merely that, as a rule, they are poorer than most. Added to that is the fact that, society, idolising them when dead, disregards its best creative talents when living. It is not difficult to determine where the artist's wife (who in history seems of less esteem than the artist's mistress) stands in social regard.

Caroline Alice Roberts has—if the paradox may be forgiven—enjoyed no posthumous life at all. She has flitted across the musicological landscape either as the "good wife" (of Malvern, Hereford, and Hampstead), submissive, tactful, dutifully inspiring; or as the lady of propriety whose starched opinions and intellectual limitations were a severe handicap to the full development of her husband's personality and desires.

The slave to duty, the "woman behind the man", was packaged for posterity by an obituarist in the *Daily Telegraph* on 10 April 1920:

> She "laid out" his scores, copied in the voice parts, planned the barring—all this for several thousands of pages of forty-five scores; the score of "The Music Makers", for instance, alone contains 150 pages of thirty-one lines.

Otherwise, noticing that she wrote some lyrics which Edward set to music, the memorialist usually footnotes Alice as one who was well-born but "married beneath her", and spent the rest of her life in repairing the damage thus done by urging her man to pull himself up the ladder down which she had come. The daughter of a Lady, she ultimately achieved Ladyship. After her death Edward, broken-hearted, never again composed a significant work.

The woman's magazine tale of heroic self-denial and immolation has of late years been somewhat reconstructed by certain persons who have had their own reasons for wishing to revise accepted opinion. Whether they were entitled to be is not the issue, but both "Dorabella" and Rosa Burley certainly were bitchy in respect of Alice Elgar.

However the matter is looked at, Alice deserves a better deal than mostly she has had. Either the inspirational force plus wifely companion thesis deserves further scrutiny; or the woman in her own right principle should be applied to one whose own gifts were closely linked to those of a national cultural hero. We have, however, to consider two women. The story of Alice Roberts lies in one compartment; that of Alice Elgar in another. The second is the sadder story, the first by far the more important, and hitherto mostly hidden from view.

In youth Alice tried the classic escape route for women imprisoned by the familial social contract of Victorian England, by writing her way towards spiritual identity. She studied science and trod in the outfield of geological scholarship, where she learned literary techniques through the disciplines of proofreading and index-making. She became poet and novelist and her ambitions grew as her interests widened. She studied music and wrote lyrics of which the best were tailor-made for setting. Like Mrs. Henry Wood—a native of Worcester, which provides a background for many of her works—Alice was (at her most lively) an acute observer of the middle class, and *Isabel Trevithoe* and *Marchcroft Manor* merit careful reading on this account. In fact, both books need to be looked at twice; for, beneath the pleasures and privileges of the well-to-do, urges of political rebelliousness are apparent. "Voulez-vous m'aider à réformer ces petits déguenillés que nous avons vu hier?'"[1] Alice was the great-granddaughter of Robert Raikes, whose sentiments these were when face to face with social malaise and deprivation, and some of his spirit informed her early ideals. She was also aware of other reforming impulses, as, for instance, from Charles Kingsley, Angela Burdett-Coutts, and Octavia Hill. Alice Roberts was herself, and the integrity of her own personality and its later transmutation remain for posterity in a heap of papers which represent her dash for freedom. These papers,[2] as well as other material, were given to me by Alice's daughter, Carice Elgar Blake, in the hope that some day I would fulfil her own wish. Carice indeed once began to write about her mother, and an orphan sheet of prologue exists:

> So much has been, and will be, written about my father that it seems only right that there should be an account of my mother and a record of the great devotion and self-sacrifice of her life to him—a record which may have been equalled but can hardly have been surpassed in human history. I have tried to give a picture of her early life and to show what a tremendous step she took when she decided to marry my father—comparatively unknown and coming from an entirely different sphere of life—time has shown that her intimation was right and her faith in his genius entirely justified—but the faith and love and self-sacrifice with which she carried through her task, congenial though it was, are things which call for admiration and should be set down for all to read.

It is my hope that the ensuing account is an adequate response to Carice's injunction, to "do for Mother what you have done for Father". It is at all events largely based on Alice's own words, and if it serves to destroy the latest televisual ploy, of presenting the first of the Enigma Variations as perpetually presiding over afternoon tea on sunlit Malvern lawns, it will have served one useful purpose. Elgar is said in music to represent England. What his wife left, and what is available in manuscript and illustration, helps one to focus on the England they knew, but which is no longer. In truth the Elgars were Victorians.

P.M.Y.

[1] *Robert Raikes et ses Ecoliers*, trs. H. Laune, Paris 1881, p. 6.

[2] Manuscripts reproduced in this book have been reduced according to the space available.

intérieures, ces pierres dégringolées que nous avons vu fuir?" Alice was the great-grandniece of Robert Raikes,[1] whose sentiments these were which came to face with stoic [illegible] and deprivation—and some of his spirit informed her mentality. She is also aware of other [illegible] impulses, as for example from Charles Kingsley, Angela Burdett-Coutts and Octavia Hill. Alice Roberts was herself, and the [illegible] of her own personality and its later transmutation remain for posterity in a heap of papers which represent her [illegible] for [illegible]. These papers, as well as other materials, were given to me by Alice's daughter, Carice Elgar Blake, in the hope that some day I would fulfil her own wish, which Carice [illegible] once began to write about her mother, of which a [illegible] of prologue exists.

So much has been, and will be, written about Elgar that it seems only right that there should be an attempt [illegible] to record the great devotion and self-sacrifice of her life—a record which may have been equalled but can hardly have been surpassed in human history. I have tried to give a picture of Alice's life and to show with what [illegible] she stepped into [illegible] when she decided to marry my father—completely unknown and coming from an entirely different sphere of life. Time has shown that her [illegible] was right, and her faith in his genius entirely justified. In the [illegible] and [illegible] with which she carried through her task [illegible] it was, are those which call for admiration and should be [illegible] afterward.

It is my hope that the [illegible] [illegible] to Carice's [illegible]: "[illegible] what you [illegible]." It is at all events [illegible] [illegible]. [illegible] deserves to dispel the [illegible] of [illegible] the first [illegible] presiding over [illegible] of [illegible]. It will have served one good purpose. [illegible] music to represent England. What his wife left, and [illegible] in [illegible] and illustration, helps [illegible] on the England [illegible] which [illegible] no longer. In truth the Elgars were Victorians.

P.M.Y.

[1] Robert Raikes of [illegible], ed. H. [illegible] (1935), p. [illegible].

Manuscripts reproduced in this book have been reduced according to [illegible] available.

I

Empire Builders

A respectable pedigree, whether for humans or animals, was a much prized asset in Victorian times, and if one was not immediately available it was necessary either to find or to invent one. The Roberts family, of Redmarley D'Abitot, Gloucestershire, in the middle of the last century were naturally concerned for the quality of their origins, and these became even more important when the daughter of the house decided to marry an impecunious musician named Edward Elgar. For then—for the benefit of the neighbourhood and an extended family—the appurtenances of inherited dignity (including "a lion rampant between two pheons, all countercharged") had to be spread over an interloper into the familiar tradition.

Caroline Alice Roberts was the daughter of Major General Henry Gee and Julia Maria Roberts, each of whom carried antecedents both interesting and impressive. By leisurely processes of research enviable credentials were produced, which led back by devious ways even to the royal Plantagenets. It is sufficient here to pick up the maternal line of descent (which most interested Alice) in 1694 when Sir John D'Oyly, of Chislehampton, Oxfordshire, married Susanna, daughter and heiress of Sir Thomas Putt, of Devonshire, and his wife Ursula, who belonged to the Cholmleys of Yorkshire. Among the offspring of the D'Oylys a daughter, Cholmley, married William Jones (d. 1779), of Nass, Gloucestershire, in 1735. Alas for this pair, for in 1772 they gained unhappy notoriety when one of their daughters, Mary, was murdered by a William Morgan. Tried and convicted at the Gloucester Assizes on 11 March, and duly executed, Morgan left a last contrite letter to his father which was included in the history of the affair published by Robert Raikes (1735–1811), a Gloucester printer who has his own place in the Elgar story. The eldest son of the Jones's, Roynon (1738–1817), married his cousin, also named Mary (d. 1808), and between 1763 and 1783 they produced thirteen children. Of the sons, William (1766–97) went into the army, rising to the rank of Lieutenant-Colonel in the 39th Regiment before his premature death while on service in the West Indies. Susanna (1767–1830)—next in the family—married into the army and her husband, George Henry Mason, was gazetted Lieutenant-Colonel too, in 1801. It is, however, two other girls of the household, Anne, born in 1763, and Margaret, six years younger, who provide the most interest.

After 1779 the girls lived at Hay Hill House, Newnham, which their father had built to accommodate his numerous brood. On 28 November 1785 Anne married John Probyn, son of Edmund Probyn, of Newland House, whose accumulation of distinction and wealth was of advantage to their descendants for many years to come. Probyn, born in 1757, a graduate of Christ Church, Oxford, was ordained into the Church of England. In 1794 he became Rector of Abinghall and Vicar of Newland, which benefices he held jointly until 1837. In 1796, however, he undertook the duties of Dean and Archdeacon of Llandaff, which he conveniently and piously could perform without leaving Gloucestershire. He retained the appointments at Llandaff until his death in 1843. For the last forty years of his life he had also borne the further responsibility of being Vicar of Matherne with Caerwent, in Monmouthshire. Heir to the Manor of Longhope, gently placed between May Hill and the Forest of Dean, Probyn there lived the life of a country gentleman and brought up a family of six children. The fourth of these, Caroline—born on 16 April 1790—married Rev. Robert Napier Raikes (1783–1851), of whose children there survived also a reasonable quiverful, of six sons and four daughters. A number of Probyns—several named John—are the subjects of pious inscriptions in the parish church at Longhope.

If Alice Roberts was impressed by the putative descent on one side from English royalty she should have been even more impressed by the supposed derivation of the Roberts's from Ynyr, King of Gwent, through the Proberts of Pant-glas. In fact she never recorded this supposition, nor—for some unexplained reason—did she ever concern herself with the Roberts dynasty which also began to assume significance during the seventeenth century. Drybridge House, opposite the road to Monmouth Castle, was built in 1628 by "William Roberts gent". The house remained in family possession, and in 1671 was graciously re-built by William Roberts, grandson of the last named, who, having been educated at Gray's Inn, became Receiver and Pay-master of the Works at Windsor Castle. In the next generation a third William Roberts became an officer in Queen Anne's army and saw service in Spain; one cousin became a barrister, another a Clerk in Holy Orders and Vicar of Framsden, in Suffolk, and a third, Thomas, a surgeon. The two sisters of William III, Elizabeth (the first Monmouth lady to keep her own carriage) and Mary, lived in Drybridge House which, after their death, passed to a cousin, Rev. William Roberts, husband of Anne Gee, daughter of the Rector of Moulton, Suffolk. The eldest son of this union was yet another William Roberts. A year after Anne Jones became Anne Probyn, this Roberts entered Pembroke College, Cambridge. In his twenty-second year—in 1788—he graduated as B.A., becoming M.A. three years later. On 11 July 1791 he was incorporated as a member of Merton College, Oxford, where he was granted the degree of Bachelor of Medi-cine on 7 July 1792.

The document testifying to this—in Latin, but with an English translation conveniently attached—was proudly preserved by Roberts's descendants. In English it runs as follows:

> The Chancellor Masters and Scholars of the University of Oxford to our beloved in Christ William Roberts, Batchelor of Medicine of Merton College in the University aforesaid, everlasting Greeting in the Lord.
>
> Whereas all our studies purposes and actions ought to be applied to the glory of God and the welfare of our brethren; and whereas Medicine among other arts, greatly conduces thereto, therefore it is that we the Chancellor Masters and Scholars aforesaid (on account of the conviction which we entertain of your science and the integrity of your life and morals) do grant to you by the tenour of these presents the free power and faculty of practising in medicine and doing all things which to such faculty belong, everywhere throughout the realm of England perpetually to continue.
>
> We also the Chancellor Masters and Scholars aforesaid bare [*sic*] witness that the before mentioned William Roberts hath

taken the oath for the primacy of the royal Majesty, and subscribed as well to all the articles of faith and religion as to those three articles comprised in Canon 36 of the Book of Constitutions and ecclesiastical canons edited in the Synod held at London in 1603 and in the first year of the reign of our Lord James etc.

For the greater faith and fuller testimony of all which things We have caused the Common Seal of the University of Oxford which we use in this behalf to be affixed to these presents.

Given at the House of our Congregation the seventh day of the month of July in the year of Our Lord 1792.

Two and a half years later Roberts was married to Margaret Jones, sister of Anne Probyn. The Marriage Licence Allegation, dated 24 January 1795, described him as of the Town of Monmouth, his bride-to-be of the Parish of Churchdown.[1] The Minutes of the General Court and Weekly Board of Gloucester Infirmary for 31 December 1795 recorded an application from Roberts for the vacant post of physician. Roberts supplemented his application with a letter to a member of the appointing body, John Parsons, of Kem[m]erton:

Gloucester Jan 4 1796

Sir,
Having, by the encouragement of numerous friends fixed my residence in this City, and tendered my services to your General Infirmary in the realm of your late Physician Dr. Hicks—I shall consider myself particularly honoured by your Interest and Support on Thursday the fourteenth instant which is fixed for the day of Election.

I have the honour to be, Sir,
Your very Hble Servt
Wm. Roberts[2]

Roberts's canvassing was effective and the *Gloucester Journal* of 18 January noted his election to the post of physician four days previously.[3]

Roberts was now happily situated. He held a position of importance and some honour, which would seem to guarantee respectability in later life. He was able to live in some style in

[1] Gloucester Diocesan Archives/transcripts/Churchdown Church Register; Q3/81.
[2] Gloucestershire Record Office, D214/F1/161.
[3] Gloucestershire Record Office, HS/B6.

Chosen House, in the parish of Churchdown,[4] in consequence of his marriage. In May 1796 a daughter, Elizabeth Cholmley, who was baptised in Churchdown on 27 May,[5] was born to the Roberts's. The eldest son, predictably named William, was born on 12 January 1798. In due course he became a solicitor with a practice in Coleford, where he rejoiced in the titles of Master Extraordinary in Chancery and one of the Perpetual Commissioners and Fire and Life Office Agent.[6] On 2 April 1799 a second daughter, Margaret, was born, who later married Thomas Probyn, a son of Archdeacon Probyn and a Captain in the service of the Honourable East India Company. Henry Gee Roberts came next, born at Chosen House on 18 July 1800, and christened in St. Michael's Church, Gloucester. Another boy, Charles, followed on 12 February 1803, after which were three girls, all bearing familiar family names: Susanna in 1804, Mary in 1806, and Ann. The last was born on 15 April 1808, five months before the death of her father: a monument in Brockworth Church, also near Chosen House, where he and his widow after him were buried reads:

> Sacred to the Memory of William Roberts, M.B., of the City of Gloucester, one of the Physicians of the General Infirmary of this County. Eldest Son of the late William Roberts of Drybridge near

[4] Susanna[h] Jones (d. 29 January 1814), sister of Roynon, married Richard Colchester, of Chosen House, a building from about the sixteenth century—to which by the nineteenth century were attached a coach-house, cottage or entrance lodge, gardens, orchard, paddock, the nearby land known as Crumps Orchard—destroyed in 1966 when the hamlet of which it was part—Hucclecote—was submerged in suburban Gloucester. After Susannah's death the property passed to Richard Colchester, then to Margaret Roberts (1799–1880), and after her marriage to John Major. On 28–29 June 1838, after having also been in the hands of one Mr. Green, the estate was acquired by Major George Watts, of Flaxley Grange, Newnham. Two sons of Roynon Jones were recorded as having died at Chosen House: Edward (1772–1847) and John (1783–1840). Chosen House was transferred to the parish of Hucclecote when this was separately established in 1851.

[5] Church Register, as (1).

[6] In 1874 William Roberts copied family particulars from a notebook, containing information in a Family Bible, which was the property of his sister Elizabeth Cholmley [*sic*] with the note: "Taken from the Nass Bible which I sent to Brockworth, March 26th, 1815": Gloucestershire Record Office D23a/28.

Monmouth. He died on the 28th of Sept. 1808 in the 42nd year of his age.[7]
Also of Mary Ann Roberts daughter of Henry Roberts and Henzey his wife who was buried on the 20th Feb. 1809 in the 14th year of her age.[8]
In Memory of Margaret Roberts relict of William Roberts, M.B., of Gloucester, daughter of the late Roynon Jones Esq. of Hay Hill in this County. She died the 7th day of July 1843 aged 73 years.

Returning to the Raikes family, it is to be noted that Robert Napier Raikes was the son of Robert Raikes, the printer already named, who has his own not inconsiderable place in history because of his concern for the poor, and his energetic promotion of educational opportunity for the children of the underprivileged in schools held on Sundays. These were not quite "Sunday Schools" (as the term later came to be understood and with the invention of which Raikes was credited), but classes in which some children, at least, could come to terms with basic literacy. Robert Napier Raikes was a student of Oriel College, Oxford, and after graduation became Vicar of Gayton with Lynn, in the diocese of Norwich. He also held the Rectory of Hellesdon with Drayton in the same diocese, where, on 11 July 1815—three weeks after the Battle of Waterloo, his daughter Julia Maria was born.

In 1837 Raikes returned to Gloucestershire, as Vicar of Longhope, and installed himself and his family in the Manor House. By this time Julia Maria was of marriageable age, and the claims of Henry Gee Roberts for her hand were soon favourably considered. Well settled in his profession, Roberts was not without some means, and he was also connected by marriage to the Probyn dynasty.

Henry Gee Roberts, who had been left fatherless at the age of eight, was, it would seem, no scholar, and in 1818 he joined the East India Company as a Cadet. This Company had then been profitably concerned with India for almost two centuries. By 1800 it had to some extent been brought under government

[7] Buried on 5 October, Brockworth Church Register.

[8] Buried on 26 February, *ibid.* Doubtless Mary Ann, daughter of William's brother, Henry, a solicitor in Stourbridge, had come to Chosen House to help her bereaved aunt Margaret.

control, but even so its authority was not less than that of a present-day multinational company, and it had its own powerful military presence. Roberts passed his probationary years satisfactorily and on 11 April 1819 was upgraded to Lieutenant in the 13th Bombay Native Light Infantry. In the next two years he saw service in Ahmadabad and the Gujurat region and helped subdue the "coolies". Advancement was smooth. In July 1824 Roberts was made Captain and a year later was in command of the Resident's escort at Kutch. The Resident at that time, Major (later Sir) Henry Pottinger, allowed his young aide considerable scope and commended him for his pacification of the unruly district north of Kutch. Meanwhile, as assistant to the Resident, Roberts was learning to undertake not only military but also political responsibility. A Major in 1835 he went back to England and during his furlough of some three years he paid court to Julia Maria Raikes, whom he married on 2 May 1838. Soon afterwards Julia found herself pregnant and on a slow boat to India.

A son, Albert Henry—dutifully named for the Prince Consort—was born on 20 September 1839. He died on 6 October 1843, at Poona, where, on a hillside, a monument was erected to his brief existence. Frederic Boyd, the second son, was born on 17 July 1841, and Stanley Napier, the third, on 28 December 1844. The Certificate of Baptism prepared by Richard Edmund Tyrwhitt (of Astley Abbots in Shropshire, and Chaplain in India from 1842 to 1857) shows that Henry Gee Roberts by now was Political Agent in Kutch and living in the Residency at Bhooj.

Caroline Alice, the last of the family, was also born in India, although there is some doubt about the exact year. According to a document in the Elgar Birthplace, at Broadheath, it was 1848. Mrs. "Vera" Raikes, her niece by marriage, indicated in a letter to Alice's daughter that it was 1849.[9] The daughter herself in her notes towards a biography of her father gave 9 October

[9] In an undated letter (after 9 April 1922) Mrs. Veronica Raikes wrote to Carice Elgar (Blake): "I was born in 1853 . . . your mother 4 years older than I was. . . ." In another letter Mrs. Raikes said that she thought that Stanley Napier "was about 2 or 3 years older" than his sister Alice. On the fly-leaf of the 1917 Diary kept by the Elgars Edward noted "C.A.E. b. Oct. 9 1848".

Major H. G. Roberts, *aet.* thirty-six or thirty-seven, at Woolwich.

1850 as the precise date of her mother's birth. This last, however, is certainly wrong, for a drawing of Hazeldine House, in Redmarley D'Abitot—the family home from 1850—done by Julia Roberts is dated 3 July 1850. It was in this year that Roberts purchased this property against his retirement and, for the time being at least, as a base from which the proper education of his sons could be organised. The education of a daughter was a matter of lesser concern.

Roberts made steady progress, that was not always unspectacular, in his profession, by playing his part in the rapid and ruthless implementation of an imperialist policy. On his return to India after his marriage he raised a regiment of irregular cavalry in Gujurat (the 11th N.I.), which he commanded until 1841. In 1843—a sad year in that Margaret Roberts died on 7 July in Cheltenham a few months before the death of her son's first-born—he was a Lieutenant-Colonel active in the campaign on the northern frontier in which Sir Charles Napier—by what he himself described as "a good, honest piece of rascality", brought recalcitrant amirs to heel and the province of Sind into British possession. The most important battle in this campaign was fought on 17 February at Miani, where Napier's force of 2,000 men encountered an army said to have been ten times larger. At this juncture, Roberts won additional esteem in that, in command at Sukkur, he seconded some of his own best troops to aid Napier. This action, Napier was reported to have said, was decisive, and he later gave it as his opinion that Roberts was the best officer in the Bombay Army, one of the best in all India, and "capable of commanding any Army in the field". Promoted Colonel of the 21st N.I. on 24 February 1852, and Major-General on 25 November 1854, Roberts was near the top of his profession. Sir Henry Bartle Frere, Chief Commissioner in Sind at this time was eloquent on the subject of Roberts's prowess, observing how he

> used the influence acquired as a daring sportsman and as a successful soldier to give the wretched people about him their first experience of power and for other purposes than tyranny and oppression and of intelligence directed to protect the right and punish the wrong doer.[10]

[10] Quoted in Gloucestershire Record Office D23a/28.

Roberts was aware of a succession of military conquests, the acquisition by the British of one province after another, the spread of modern communications and the implementation of some reforms in the subjugated territories, and a growing impatience on the part of the indigenous population with foreign insistence on changes in long established ways of life. In May 1857, insurrection broke out at Meerut and soon spread to Delhi. Before long the whole Ganges valley was in turmoil. What was in fact a war of liberation came temporarily to an end when the native fighters came to realise that for the time being at least the occupying power was too formidable to dislodge.

Ever since 1850 Roberts had been looking forward to retirement, but his final departure from the Bombay Army was delayed time after time, although he was often in England on leave. In the end he was caught up with the so-called Mutiny and its aftermath, which brought an end to the power of the old East India Company and the transference of its authority to the Crown. Still active in the field, Roberts was in command of the Rajputana Field Force that took Kotah and seventy-eight guns by assault, in March 1858, and helped in the harrying of Tantia Topi, "the only rebel leader who showed a real genius for war". Roberts defeated the so-called rebel soldiers at Sanganir, at Kankrauli, on the Banas (Rajputana), on 14 August 1858, but in the end it was a junior officer, a Major Meade, who captured Tantia Topi on 7 April 1859. Eleven days later, after a form of trial, Topi was executed. He was, it was said, "cruel and crafty".

In the intervening period Roberts, who was now home for good, was among those included in a Parliamentary motion of thanks approved in the House of Commons on 14 April.

> *Resolved, Nemine Contradicente,* That the Thanks of this House be given to General the Right honourable Lord *Clyde*, G.C.B., Commander-in-Chief in *India*; Lieutenant-General Sir *James Outram*, Baronet, G.C.B.; Major-General Sir *Hugh Henry Rose*, G.C.B.,; Major-General *Henry Gee Roberts*; Major-General *George Cornish Whitlock;* Major-General Sir *Archdale Wilson*, Baronet, K.C.B., Major-General Sir *James Hope Grant*, K.C.B.; Major-General Sir *William Rose Mansfield*, K.C.B.; Major-General Sir *Thomas Harte Franks*, K.C.B.; Major-General Sir *Edward Lugard*, K.C.B.; Major-General Sir *John Michael*, K.C.B.; Brigadier-General *Robert Walpole*, C.B.; Brigadier-General Sir *Robert Napier*, K.C.B.;

and Captain *Edward Sotheby*, R.N., C.B., for the eminent skill, courage and perseverance displayed by them during the military operations by which the late Insurrection in *India* has been effectually suppressed.

As a further recognition of his services Roberts was created a Knight Commander of the Bath.

The influence of India was very strong on the Roberts household. Julia Maria was able not only to rejoice in the valorous exploits of her husband, but also in the careers of her six brothers, all of whom joined the East India Company. The most distinguished was Robert Napier Raikes (II) who, thirteen years younger than Roberts, made equally steady and satisfactory progress. Commissioned in the 67th Bengal Native Infantry, Raikes transferred to the 1st Gwalior Cavalry, "in which he saw his first active service, in the form of rebel and dacoit hunting in Bundelkund".[11] He fought in various theatres, helped to put down the "Mutiny", and in the subsequent pacification (because of his knowledge of horses) was Remount Agent for Upper India. Raikes ended his career as a General, and his life, in his ninety-seventh year, in his native Gloucestershire.

The youngest of the brothers, Stanley Napier, was born in 1824. In 1858 he married Arabella Veronica James, of Newnham-on-Severn, a grand-daughter of General John Dighton on her father's side, and of Dean Probyn on her mother's. Veronica (later known to the family at large as Aunt Vee) had a five-year-old daughter (Vera) at the time of her second marriage. This took place in India where Stanley Napier was with his regiment and she was escorted there by Fred Roberts, who was joining his regiment. Stanley Napier Raikes left the Indian Army with the rank of Colonel, and in his later years he served as a Justice of the Peace in Gloucestershire. He died in 1891 and was buried in Dymock churchyard. Mrs. Raikes lived to the age of ninety-six, her death occurring in 1923.

Longevity was a characteristic of the Raikes's. Julia's sisters Caroline and Gertrude both lived on into ripe old age, outlasting not only Julia but also her daughter Alice. In 1841 Caroline married Captain John Henry Dighton, another Indian Army officer, whose family exercised much influence in the Forest of

[11] *The Globe*, 19 February 1909.

Dean. In 1847 Gertrude married Sir Thomas Raikes Trigge Thompson, Bart., a Vice-Admiral in the Royal Navy. After his death in 1865 Lady Thompson kept her sights firmly trained on the younger members of the families with which she had the closest connections. Misdemeanours, of which marrying out of one's class was, perhaps, the chief, caught her ire.

Mrs. Dighton and Lady Thompson exercised a terrifying influence over successive generations. The former (known to the family as Aunt "Car") lived in Oak House, in Newland, and specialised in a brusque manner that caused her younger daughter to leave home as soon as she could. Lady Thompson had two daughters, Gertrude and Emily. Gertrude stayed by her mother's side, doing as she was told. Emily, on the other hand, went completely off course to become a social worker in the Paddington district of London. In later life, Lady Thompson regarded it as her social duty (and that of Gertrude) to visit poor relations including the Elgars.

The boys whom Henry Gee Roberts had sent home were duly conditioned to follow in their father's footsteps. A College was established in Cheltenham primarily for the purpose of educating the sons of the military. The neighbourhood was plentifully sprinkled with families of serving and retired officers, and—in increasing numbers—also of officials in the Government of India. The College hopefully began as an institution with a strong classical bias. But it became apparent that not all sons of army officers were conspicuous by reason of their enthusiasm for Latin and Greek. Accordingly a Civil and Military Department was founded to accommodate the less academic. Although the administration of the College was rather cumbersome the intention was more or less that of a comprehensive school for the high-class. There was a Principal, whose responsibility it was to safeguard the intellectual integrity of the school, a Head Master of the Civil and Military Department, and—although these worthies were both at the time of consideration in Holy Orders—two Theological Tutors to inculcate the proper Christian doctrines. Discipline was—literally—in the hands of "The Discipline Committee", in fact a sub-committee—for whose active service there were always available well-experienced volunteers —of the Board of Directors who ran the place for the first eighteen years as a proprietary institution. Many of the teaching staff, it may be said, had connections of one sort or another with the Indian sub-continent.

The Roberts boys were admitted to the school when Rev. William Dobson, a former classical Fellow of Trinity College, Cambridge, was Principal, and the Rev. Thomas Southwood superintended the "modern" studies of the Civil and Military Department. Frederic entered in August 1852, and was regarded as a Boarder. Stanley Napier—henceforth known in the family as Napier—was admitted as a Day Boy in August 1858. (At that time his parents had a *pied à terre* in Cheltenham.) Neither boy won a prize and neither was in the school cricket team.

Fred was able to overlap his father's career in the Indian Army, joining the Bombay Artillery, by Direct Commission, as a 2nd Lieutenant in 1857. He became a 1st Lieutenant in 1858, a Captain in the Royal Artillery in 1866, and a Major in 1877. Napier became an Ensign in the 104th Foot in 1863 after attendance at the Royal Military Academy, Sandhurst. Passing through the various qualifying grades he became a Major in the Liverpool Regiment in 1882. He fought in India, in Afghanistan, and in Burma, and won several medals. After retirement Napier Roberts joined the ranks of the superannuated in Cheltenham.

The Roberts's were in at the beginning of the imperial part of Indian history, and being in at the beginning were also in at the beginning of the end. Terrible things happened, and no doubt they were not unaware of such hideous treatment as in the transport of slave labour from one place to another, as trade demanded. In 1865 nearly 6,000 Indian labourers were transported to the West Indies.

> Yet this humane and profitable consumption of the surplus labour of the East, an interchange so beneficial to both parties, is so little understood in many parts of England as to be looked upon as but a shade removed from slavery.[12]

But for those who carried the burden of empire there were also disillusionments.

> . . . all may be dearly bought—a state of personal restriction against which independent feeling revolts, precious years of youth

[12] *Chambers's Journal*, 1866, p. 397.

sacrificed, long years of exile among barbarians in a climate which is for the most part adverse to comfort, and destructive of human life, and the possibility of returning home when past middle life with a diseased liver, to find your old friends dead and gone, and yourself a stranger in the land of your birth.[13]

In the end Major-General Roberts only went home to die. The victim of cancer of the throat, he spent a brief year among the woodlands around his estate and in the fine house he had furnished with the Indian furniture, ornaments, and trophies he had brought back from time to time when on leave. He died on 6 October 1860 and was buried just outside the north wall of the nave of Redmarley Church. On the inside of the same wall is a commemorative tablet epitomising his career and carrying his coat of arms with motto: *Fortiter et fide.* The same device was ultimately placed on the gravestone of his daughter Alice.

[13] *ibid.*, 1868, p. 343.

Julia Roberts and her sons, Frederic and Stanley, October 1846.
Watercolour by Mrs Henry Moseley.

A grave in India.
Artist unknown:

2

Growing up in Redmarley D'Abitot

Redmarley D'Abitot was an ideal place in which patriots and patricians might live at ease. Lying under the Malvern Hills and standing lonely amid richly cultivated fields, it has a quiet scenic originality that may be taken to represent the true image of pastoral England. This is so even now. Since so little seemingly has changed in the last hundred years it might be thought that history has passed this village by. In fact, history, in one sense, ended here; for in few places which are so tiny is there so much in view.

The Roman legions came by this way and their passage is marked by places where their discarded pottery was lately discovered. As the name signifies the Normans came here too. They stayed to incorporate the neighbouring countryside into the royal hunting preserve of Malvern Chase. Hunting has had an unbroken history since the Middle Ages, and in the days of the Roberts's, Mastership of the Ledbury Fox Hounds was a position much sought after. There was also good partridge and mixed shooting, fishing for trout in the Leadon—the little river running beneath the village—and for salmon in the not too distant Wye at Hereford or Ross.

In its time Redmarley knew violence. Skirmishes in the Wars of the Roses took place in its fields and in 1644 a battle between Cavaliers and Roundheads was fought there, between 3 and 8 August. As to how the battle started there were a number of legends. One account stated that a number of workers were cutting wheat in the fields by Hazeldine—the estate that was to become the property of the Roberts's—when cannon balls began flying above their heads. Be that as it may, there was a general alarm and the villagers quickly evacuated their cottages and took to the comforting woods. More than two hundred years later, on 10 February 1885, an old woman named Anne

Hardman told how it had been handed down in her family that when her ancestors living in those turbulent days returned to their home they found it "over their shoes in blood".[1] A farm named Redhill is also supposed to commemorate that gory fact. The church registers record the burial of seventeen who were slain in the battle of Redmarley.

Two centuries later the calm tenor of life was disturbed by the establishment of an agricultural cooperative, inspired by the Chartist leader, Feargus O'Connor, at the nearby townland of Lowbands, where the tradition was kept in the memory by the so-called "Chartists' Cottages", built in 1847. Near here a Dissenting Chapel was built, also as a token of radicalism.

The centre of life was the church. Dedicated to St. Bartholomew, this was first built in the twelfth or thirteenth century. Of the original fabric nothing remains. The fine Perpendicular tower (temporarily pinnacle-less) is of the fifteenth century, but the main body of the edifice is Victorian. The Registers, however, go back to the early sixteenth century, and there is a silver chalice, dated 1571, which was presented to the church by Elizabeth I in token of the hospitality she received during one of her progresses. During the eighteenth century the six bells which still ring harmoniously from the tower were made for the church by Abraham Rudhall, of Gloucester, and their message runs as follows:

Reap wheat and mow barley,
Say the bells of Redmarley.

In the tower area there is a fine churchwardens' chest of 1757, the wardens at that time being Will. Terrett and Thomas Hendy.

The story of Redmarley Church overlaps that of Hardy's Mellstock, and the activities of the musicians who used to accompany the metrical psalms and newer hymns are enshrined in one of the Account Books of 1834.

April	4	1 Bass Viol string	1/4
	11	2 Violin strings	1/0
May	6	3 „ „	1/0
June	2	1 Set of strings	1/10

[1] Rev. H. M. Niblett compiled a history of the parish (dated "Whitsuntide 1891"), of which the MS. remains in the custody of the church.

August	9	1 Violin String	/4
		2 " "	1/0
		Bass Viol 3rd string	1/4
Sept.	5	Violin string	/3

On the south-west of the church and right beside the graveyard is the old "Workhouse", one of a number of houses in the neighbourhood dating from the seventeenth century, or earlier. Across the road is another such building, the former Post House. Here the four-horse coach running daily from Gloucester to Hereford called, drawing up each morning somewhere between eight and nine o'clock—according to the temper of the horses and the state of the weather. Horses were changed at the Feathers at Staunton and again at Ledbury. On its return the coach put down and picked up in Redmarley at nine o'clock at night. The coach service was still running when the Roberts family acquired Hazeldine House.

At that time—in 1850—the more modest of the people of the neighbourhood lived in a state of disciplined obedience. There were many labourers, as well as carters, thatchers, basket-makers, blacksmiths, sawyers, masons, carriers, cowmen and shoemakers. One unusual trade (as described in a marriage certificate) was that of castrator. Otherwise there were gamekeepers, coach-builders and painters, millers, farmers of various grades, publicans, and tradesmen—including an earthenware dealer. There was also a postman. And a few young men, lured by the distant call of the sea, joined the navy. After 1846—when a school was opened in Lowbands, for the district between and about Redmarley and the nearby village of Pendock, after initial donations of £111 by the Rector and £50 by Lord Beauchamp—a schoolmaster (or schoolmistress) was to be found among the villagers. This was in addition to the lady who maintained a Dame School at Payford Bridge.

In the marriage registers it was not only men who were described as labourers, but also women, of whom many were simply designated "servants". Some women of the parish were employed in making gloves for Dent, Allcroft & Co., of Worcester. The agent of this firm used regularly to call at the Rose and Crown (where the Ledbury Hounds also met) on the Gloucester–Ledbury Road, to collect the finished articles. Of the working people of

Redmarley the great majority could neither read nor write, and their "marks" in the official records bear mute witness to the distance of disadvantage between the privileged few and the underprivileged many. The latter were still to be described, as on some occasions by Alice Roberts, as "peasants".

The aristocrat among the poorer section of the community was the Parish Clerk—necessarily a man endowed with some special gifts, of voice and bearing, and a degree of literacy. All the time Alice Roberts lived in Redmarley the same Clerk was in office. On 31 March 1902, which was Easter Monday, "Mr. James Brewer, the respected Clerk of the Parish died aged over 91 he held the office for 60 years universally esteemed he was buried on Saturday, April 5th".

Redmarley once made the national news on account of the longevity of one of its inhabitants. On 12 October 1868 Richard Purser, once a cowman, died at the age of 112—a direct link between the ages of Handel and Elgar!

There was a distinctive local dialect, rich and musical, and some strange transmutations of terminology took place. Redmarley D'Abitot presented opportunity for variations, and in 1546 the Parish Clerk suggested Dorbytott as an authentic orthography. The district known as Lowbands was more properly Lowburn (so written in 1830), defining the burn, or brook, by Blackford Mill. The Baccus represented "the back house", formerly the Angel Inn; Beryn stood for "bare end"; the Lezar for "leasow", or pasture. Egg's Tump was a tautology since both "egg" and "tump" were words for a hill; scar, for rock or cliff, is known in other parts of the country, particularly in Yorkshire; Cob Hill was again tautologous, for cob, or cop, meant peak. On the north side of the parish an apparatus that had once been situated there was grimly remembered in Gallows Brook. Once upon a time there was an imaginative Surveyor of Turnpikes in the area, named Stokes, who, finding a paucity of names for the purposes of topography, introduced Hyde Park Corner, Drury Lane, and Pall Mall, incongruities which amply satisfy a natural English instinct for eccentricity.

This was a country of stately homes and manor houses. Bury Court, Birtsmorton Court, Down House—where the Scobells lived, Murder House, at Berrow, home of the Morgans, Hill

Fields which the Townshends acquired in due course, the Rectory, and Hazeldine, were gracious through their evolution and setting. The Rectory—one of the newer houses—had been built in about 1744. During the next hundred and fifty years it was to be several times enlarged at considerable cost. The estate of Hazeldine belonged to John Terrett (son of William?) in 1798, to Samuel Davis in 1817, and to Samuel Beal in 1820. In 1825 Thomas Hill, Rector of Staunton, who lived at Fairfields, paid £8,968 for 154 acres and built the modestly stately home in which the Roberts's were to live. In so doing he impoverished himself and the property was in the hands of Mrs. Mary Terrett and a Trustee until 1850 when Colonel Roberts, as he then was, purchased the estate. It was in the possession of the Roberts's until 1891 when it was bought by the Misses Fenton. Apart from the family quarters which included six bedrooms, there were servants' sleeping quarters, servants' hall, and butler's pantry. Outside there was accommodation for six horses and, commanding the main entrance, a commodious lodge. After the Roberts's left the house its plain late Georgian exterior was replaced by a more pretentious "Jacobethan" covering.

Although after his acquisition of Hazeldine, Colonel Roberts was more often in India than in Redmarley, his concern for local affairs was considerable. He was, after all, among those to whom the natives would look for advice and, in times of need, succour. In the year in which his family settled into the house there were 1192 inhabitants of Redmarley; across the years there was a consistent decline in numbers so that when Alice finally disposed of Hazeldine there were only 923 people living in the village. This fact illustrates vividly the continuing elimination of small farmers and freeholders by the purchase of land by the wealthy in order to establish themselves within the company of aristocracy, and by the subtraction of labour from agriculture by the progress of industrialisation in the midland towns.

The Napoleonic Wars had seen an erosion of rural living standards through inflation, and when the Roberts's came to Redmarley there were clear evidences of decline in prosperity. The main part of the church, for example, was almost in ruins. In winter the chancel was awash with the rain-water that poured through the broken roof, and it was necessary to put boards down on which the officiating clergy could stand.

The opportunity to consider restorative measures came after the passing of Rector James Commeline in 1853. The manner of his going, like that of Elisha, was helped by a chariot of fire; for he fell asleep without extinguishing his candle one night, and never woke again. He was succeeded by Edward Henry Niblett, who was Rector until 1878. The patronage of the rectory of Redmarley had been purchased by Niblett's father, Daniel John Niblett, of Haresfield Court, Gloucestershire, and the investment proved well worthwhile in terms of careers for his family. Nibletts held the Rectory for more than a century in unbroken succession, and the patronage even longer. Edward Henry, who married Mary Anne Law, daughter of James Law Stewart, of Jamaica, in 1848, was a man of some authority when he came to Redmarley. He was not enchanted at the prospect of dealing with his parishoners, however attractive the living conditions in the splendid, manorial, Rectory. "The people," he observed, "were a rude, rough type, and the church was in ruins. . . ."

The first priority was to improve the Rectory, and in 1854 a sum of £1,457 was expended on reconditioning. Throughout E. H. Niblett's incumbency changes were made, especially in 1867 when a new bedroom and a conservatory were added. Although the Rector was not a poor man the funds for these improvements were raised on short term mortgages. It was not long before the condition of the church itself was considered. Not only was the existing building in a state of virtual nonexistence, it was too small. That, at least, was the theory, although the figures for church attendance for the rest of the century give rise to doubts on that issue. Nonetheless, the assumption that there would be more rather than less worshippers in the future impressed on Niblett the need to allow for their comfortable accommodation. So it was decided to build a new church onto the tower. A vaguely Early English manner was recommended, and on 11 July 1855 the Rector's eldest son laid the Foundation Stone. The work was done in a very short time and on 5 June 1856 St. Bartholomew's Church, Redmarley D'Abitot, was reopened. The sermon at the Morning Service was preached by Rev. W. S. Symonds, of the neighbouring parish of Pendock, and Mr. Jagg, of Eastnor, brought his choir over for the day.

The long list of Subscribers to the re-building fund gives these particulars which are of interest in the present context:

Miss Roberts	£3.0.0.
Doctor Henry	£20.0.0.
T. Gambier Parry	£50.0.0.
Misses Baker	£3.0.0.
W. [S.] Symonds	£1.0.0.
Lady Georgina Lygon	£10.0.0.
Earl Beauchamp	£100.0.0.[2]
Rev. J. Lander	£2.2.0.
General Roberts	£10.0.0.

Whether Miss Roberts represented Alice (by arrangement with her mother or a relative is not clear. Dr. Henry, of the Hall at Haffield Camp, some three miles south of Ledbury, was a friend of Symonds and mentioned in Symonds's *Records of the Rocks* (see p. 68). He may also be suspected to have been the subject of one of Alice's later fantasies.

Gambier Parry, a wealthy landowner in Gloucestershire, an ecclesiastical artist, was the father of Hubert Parry. The Misses Baker, from Hasfield Court, were friends of the Roberts's and destined to play a part in the Elgar saga. The Lygon family, of whom Beauchamp was the chief, were also to have their place in this branch of history. The Rev. W. S. Symonds and Rev. J. Lander were to be lifelong friends of Alice, and the former a particularly powerful influence on her intellectual development. John Lander (1817–93), a Gloucester man, was Rector of the tiny parish of Donnington—a leafy retreat in Herefordshire off the Ledbury–Dymock road—from 1845 to 1890.

It took another eight years for the church at Redmarley to be furnished as Niblett wished to see it. On 18 September 1864 the new organ, by Nicholson of Worcester, was dedicated, and the Rector had to make a point in his sermon of stating his sympathy with all those among the faithful who "objected to 'innovations' ". So the old instruments of the church band

[2] Lord Beauchamp also gave the porch to the church, as a separate donation.

were committed to silence and the memory of those who had played them faded as the last of them were committed to the grave.

One other building testifies to the energy of E. H. Niblett. In 1860 an "Upper School" was established in the village, near the church, to supplant that at Lowbands which was both too distant from the centre of the parish and also too small. This building at the present time is the Village Hall.

Vera (Dighton) Raikes used to visit Hazeldine in her childhood and she left some impressions in letters which she wrote in old age. Her memories, after the passage of seventy years and more, were lively.

When they took possession of their property Henry and Julia Roberts planted three trees which were named Fred, Napier, and Alice. Julia was, and remained, strong on the proprieties. Mrs. Raikes remembered

> her telling me how the "little boys" Fred and Napier used to be *dressed* before being allowed to walk with their nurse or whoever it was down into the *village* at Redmarley. Never *allowed* beyond the gates in their *garden* clothes!

There were visits from relatives, of course, and Julia's brother Stanley used to spend some of his leaves at Hazeldine. During Stanley Napier's first year at Cheltenham College his parents had a house in Cheltenham, presumably for use in term time. In front of that house Alice

> was allowed to trundle her hoop up and *down* Imperial Square . . . (but only where she could be *seen* from the windows. . . .)

Then there was a trip

> to a menagerie or as it was then I expect a "wild beast" show.
>
> At the sight of the animals & almost before entering my terror was so great that he [General Roberts] *quickly* and *so* kindly took me *at once away*. I *never* forgot it!
>
> The next recollection was *I suppose* the following year as we Uncle Stanley Aunt Vee & I were living one year at *Newnham on Severn* (where I was born), & during that time I was told [General Roberts] had *died*. I was sorry, no doubt, but *very proud*, as I was put into a little mourning . . . 2 years *later* we went to *Hill Ash* [Dymock] & from that time Hazeldine was a second home to me. I was then I think 8 years old.

In those days the cultural life of Cheltenham was enriched by a music teacher of Swedish origin. On 12 December 1863, *The Musical World* proclaimed: "Mr. von Holst has announced a musical *soirée* for Wednesday next at Hale's Music Room."

The church at Redmarley is a tiny corner of the Indian Empire. General Roberts, Julia, and Fred are commemorated there. So too are Captain W. C. Dowdeswell, a victim of cholera, and Charles Lingard Stokes, chief officer of the Locomotive Department in the Bengal Division of the East India Railway, who died on 19 January 1864. The stained glass at the western end of the north aisle was inserted in his memory.

Lady Roberts settled down in 1860 to play the role of widow according to expectation. Despite the amenities of Hazeldine she claimed only to have limited resources. Not infrequently a relative degree of poverty was imputed by such people to the improvidence (if not downright wickedness) of disreputable ancestors. Legends concerning impropriety in the family—the authors of such impropriety rarely being actually named—were an educational convenience. Thrift, truthfulness, moral uprightness (as then conceived), were often inculcated through a sense of fear. One of the notable features of the Gloucestershire countryside is May Hill, near Longhope. Lady Roberts used to say that May Hill had once been in the ownership of the family, but had been among the assets lost by one of her ancestors through gambling.

Lady Roberts possessed a little talent for sketching and two drawings of Hazeldine and its landscape by her enshrine the enduring charm of the scene, but also the frustrations of genteel widowhood in the early part of the Victorian era. Like musical accomplishment, ability in the visual arts was not to be taken too far—against which doctrine Lady Roberts's daughter was to stage her own protest. The ability to protest developed out of another of Lady Roberts's interests. The London Library had been founded in 1841 and she was among its early members. From her youth up Alice was a great reader, and she even looked forward to becoming a great writer.

There were, however, duties to be performed. Lady Roberts was said to have been prominent in promoting charitable ventures and to have established a particular fund for the alleviation of poverty and distress. Carice Elgar Blake recorded how (in the 1930's?)

> there was a woman still living near [Redmarley] Church who remembers going to Hazeldine House with her mother to pay money into a club founded by my Grandmother to help the poor. Her chief recollection seemed to be the rustle of her ladyship's silk dress which evidently impressed her deeply.

Among the other duties one of the most pressing was the giving and receiving of visiting cards and consolidation of the consequent rituals of hospitality thereby imposed. This is set out in Alice's novel, *Marchcroft Manor*, of 1882, in this manner:

> De Tressanay turned over the cards which had accumulated in the old china bowl on the hall table.
>
> "We will drive and return some of these visits," he said, "and leave invitations to some of the people for luncheon on the day of the flower show."

The aim of such exchanges of hospitality was the preservation of amity among the principal families of the neighbourhood. Since there was so much intermarriage and so many strong feelings in respect of orders of precedence this was not always quite easy. Nevertheless there was unanimity on one issue, that was as to how the lower classes, and also children, should behave. The poor illiterate labourers of both sexes whose 'marks' abide as pathetic tributes to their deprivation were expected to show respect. Those who had spent their lives in disciplining Indian peasants were not altogether disposed to forget the principles on which they had depended in exile. As she grew older, Lady Roberts was more rather than less inclined to continue the military procedures into which she had married.

There were servants who won their place in family affections. They knew their places.

According to Vera Raikes,

> There was a very important and much *respected maid* called *Rundle,* devoted to them [the children] *in reality* but *severe.*
>
> She said [Alice] who was gentle & good to a degree had "a bad a *fearful* bad disposition". Napier used to call her "Rundle tundle" & when I married she was deeply interested, & signified

her approval by *saying*—"Nice dresses, good jewelry & all *as it should be*!" (with hands folded).

Those women who spent their lives ("with hands folded") in domestic service properly earned the qualification which was customarily bestowed on them. Sarah Allen too was a "devoted" maid,

> who began her service as a very young girl at Hazeldine House & who nursed [Lady Roberts] in her last illness & remained with my Mother until she married. Later on she came back to us & was the greatest comfort. We all felt as long as she was there everything would be perfectly all right. She remained with us after my Mother's death but became a victim of a most painful form of neuritis & died in 1923.[8]

In Redmarley there is still the ghost of a memory of Lady Roberts. Old Anne Hardman—who recollected the legends of the Civil War—used to tell her family how Lady Roberts would stand in the street outside her house and peremptorily call out "Anne Hardman", and expect immediate response.

It was a misfortune for any girl like Alice to be an only daughter. The likeliest destiny was a desiccated spinsterhood, taken through long years of dutiful companionship to the widowed mother into a final period of desolation and segregation. While her brothers were being schooled at the College in Cheltenham Alice was put under the regimen of governesses. The prospects for governesses as also for their pupils were indicated in an advertisement disapprovingly cited by the Editor of *Jerrold's Magazine*, IV, 1846, as "The most *naïve* and altogether perfect expression of rapacity and intense selfishness we have ever met with":

> TO GOVERNESSES AND OTHERS:—Wanted, by an English family (living in Scotland) an active, cheerful, and obliging YOUNG LADY, who is competent to take the charge of education, and otherwise, of three children, all under six years of age; also make herself generally useful in domestic matters. This is required in return for her board, lodging, washing, etc., but if on all other points an applicant should suit, a small salary would not be refused, if particularly wanted. As the advertiser and her mother have the children constantly with them, the governess will necessarily live in the bosom of the family: lady-like manners and

[8] From Carice Elgar Blake's MS.

address are therefore indispensable. French, music (vocal and instrumental), drawing, dancing needlework, English, etc., will gradually be required. The situation is likely to be permanent, and certainly comfortable and advantageous. Most unexceptionable references will be given and required.

In due course, in *Marchcroft Manor*, Alice made her own estimate of the value of the kind of education allowed to the daughters of the class to which she belonged. In respect of Ella and Olive Malloney (motherless daughters of a doctor)

No pains had been spared to make their education complete. Masters and mistresses had succeeded the governess as the time for "finishing their education" drew near; yet when they left the schoolroom, the instruction which had been expended on them with so much pains seemed to have either vanished to a great extent, or else, with the same outer effect, it had sunk too deeply into their systems to rise and shine on the surface.

Alice was a lively—at times even an obstreperous child. Playing with her brothers when they were at home, she learned boys' pursuits. She bowled and batted as and when they required cricket practice, and learned to ride a horse. She absorbed facts of history and of natural history simply by observing her richly detailed environment. Hazeldine was a lovely place in which to grow up, and in the gardens and shrubberies the children were taught to recognise the birds that came there. Alice became a keen bird-watcher, especially liking wrens and tits, and to set out coconut and other delicacies for birds became a lifelong discipline. Like her father she had an affection for and understanding of animals, amongst which her chief friends were horses and Persian cats. Even in girlhood she displayed other characteristics that later were to be seen as complementary to those of Edward Elgar. She had a rich vein of curiosity, and also an inventive urge. Thus, in her teens, she designed a revolving summer-house which was duly built by the village carpenter and, having read about the instrument, she insisted on having an Aeolian harp set up in the grounds.

In one way or another Alice managed to acquire a large stock of useful information. She read widely, deeply, and gained more than useful working knowledge of modern languages. Like the Malloney girls, she also acquired some skill in music. The musical experts of Redmarley when Alice was a girl were the Rector's wife, a Miss Stokes (presumably a sister of the deceased railway engineer), and the schoolmistress, who were jointly charged with the responsibility for the church organ and its use.

Some part of Alice's life reads like episodes from *Scenes of Clerical Life* (George Eliot's book was published in 1858). The broad and benevolent interests of the Rev. John Selby, of *Marchcroft Manor*, were a reflection of those of the clergy who looked after the spiritual welfare of the Roberts's and their friends in the neighbourhood of Hazeldine. John Selby, according to his niece knew everything—"architecture, history, and all". The "cool drawing-room" of the Marchcroft Rectory, "hung with paintings of landscapes and portraits, and fragrant with a profusion of flowers", was like those in the Georgian houses in which the Rectors of Redmarley and Pendock lived.

Throughout Alice's youth E. H. Niblett occupied the Redmarley Rectory. His son, Henry Morton, born in 1854, meanwhile came to manhood, for which he was duly prepared at Clifton College and Pembroke College, Oxford. He graduated in 1878 (taking his Master's degree three years later). On 20 October E. H. Niblett died and his son's intended place was kept warm by Rev. William Lewis Mills (1804–91), a Gloucestershire man with a Gloucestershire wife (Elizabeth Hayward, from Frocester Court), and a long record of service in Gloucestershire parishes. He was also author of *Recollections of Rambles in North Wales*. In 1882 Henry Morton was ready for his inheritance, and Mills gracefully retired, the new Rector being inducted on 24 May.

This Rector was zealous in his concern for the social, cultural, and charitable instincts of his parishoners. He organised the better-off to administer appropriate treatment. The schoolroom, therefore was a community library, books being available for borrowing after Morning Prayer on the second and fourth Sundays of the month on payment of ½d. per volume. On winter evenings, under Rectorial supervision, the faithful strove towards self-improvement and spiritual regeneration through bible study, and the reading of *Good Words, Home Words, Home Chimes, The Dawn of Day,* and the *Sunday Magazine.* Alice showed early tendencies towards moral supervision and a facility in the science of censorship, in the careful editing of selected passages from the works of William Shakespeare (who had known this same countryside where was John Falstaff's rural residence) and their reading aloud. For the sturdier members of the community there was encouragement to join the Young Men's and Young Women's Christian Associations, to assist—albeit at long range—to convert the heathen by undertaking needlework for the Zenana—or some other—Mission. The *Memorials of Frances Ridley Havergal*, published by James Nisbet in 1881, give another view of the spiritual temper of the people of the West Midlands among whom Miss Havergal lived during the time when Alice was growing up.

In her novel Alice introduces the reader to the "cottage garden show" and to the more extensive "Flower Show". These were great enterprises in the bright days of high summer, and most famous of all was the Eastnor Flower Show. In Redmarley the classic event was Sunday School Treat. There were tea on the Rectory lawn, at tables "given" by the lady of Bury Court, the Postmistress (whose official residence then was the former Workhouse), and other benevolent females; games in the field in front of the Rectory, where one could find a steam roundabout in the course of time, as well as swingboats, and even a rifle saloon; and music from the Staunton (or other) band. The children took part in a primitive cricket-like game, "stoolboard", and egg-and-spoon races; the women of the parish (of the inferior classes) in a game in which the aim was, when blindfolded, to pin a tail on the correct part of the anatomy of a donkey in effigy (the Rector missed an opportunity here to vary this game, for his family motto was *Sicut aquilae penis*), and in races for which the prizes were packets of tea.

Decades of treats were the tradition on which the Jubilee celebrations of 1887 were built. That year, apparently like every other in that age, June gave unblemished days of "Queen's weather", and the fields were quite brown and many trees even showing signs of drooping. On 23 June, there was a church service at 11.30, after which the day was given up to revelry. On Mr. Beach's field near the village green (this last having disappeared into somebody's estate in the years between then and now) 500 adults, having received tickets of admission beforehand, sat down to dinner in a large tent. There were games for the children, followed by tea, and dancing to the music of the 1st Gloucester Engineers Band. All this cost £60, "the principal rich inhabitants . . . willingly contributing towards it". Lord Beauchamp[4] headed the subscription list with £15 and he and his family drove over from Madresfield to signify his interest. The children went home each with a medal. Bolder spirits stayed until after the beneficed clergy and the gentry had departed to their more prosperous domesticity and the sun had gone down over the Marches.

Routines seemed then timeless and unchanging. The persons to be visited seemed ageless. Some of them, although in no way that they would have expected, have their little corner in immor-

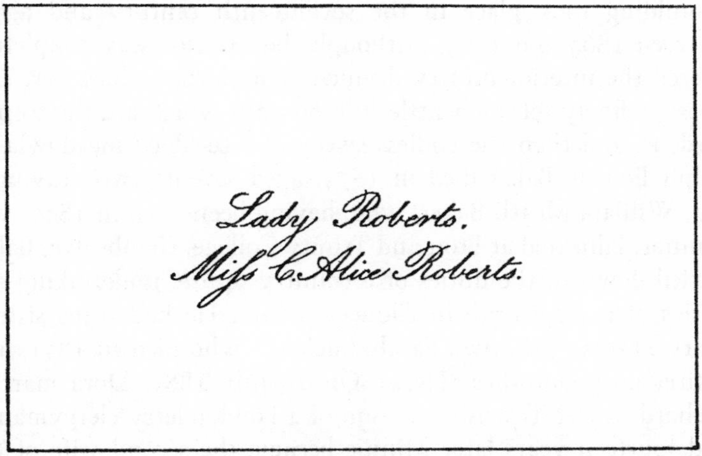

Visiting card.

tality. Among the characters in the "Enigma" Variations is W. M. B.—William Meath Baker. Had the Roberts's not numbered the Bakers of Hasfield among their acquaintances

[4] Frederick Lygon (1830–91) M.P. for Tewkesbury, 1857–63, and West Worcester, 1863–6, succeeded as sixth Earl Beauchamp in 1866. A High Churchman, who helped to found Keble College, Oxford, he compiled a Hymnal for Madresfield, where was the family seat, and where in due course his daughter Lady Mary Lygon established a Music Festival. W. H. Elgar, father of Edward, tuned the pianos at Madresfield Court.

the "Enigma" Variations would have taken a different form. It is, of course, possible that they would have taken no form at all.

The Manor of Hasfield, in the Hundred of Westminster, in the County of Gloucester, had once belonged to the Priory of Deerhurst. Having passed through a number of hands it came in 1863 into the possession of William Baker, who also owned Fenton House, in the County of Stafford. Two years later Baker died, his heir being his brother, Rev. Ralph Bourne Baker, son-in-law of the Bishop of Meath, the title of whose see was incorporated within the patronymic of the Bakers of Hasfield. Hasfield Court stood on the site of a medieval house, within a stone's throw of the village church. The oldest parts were of the sixteenth century, particularly panelling of 1558 in the former dining room. Rebuilding took place in the seventeenth century and again between 1863 and 1865. Although the exterior was completely altered the interior preserved much of its former character. The house is finely set, on a little hill, beneath which are the formal gardens, and then the endless sweep of tree-edged meadowland. Ralph Bourne Baker died in 1875, aged seventy-two, leaving a son, William Meath Baker, who, having been born in 1857, was a minor. Educated at Eton and Trinity College, Cambridge, Baker settled down to the duties of a country squire, undertaking the duties of a magistrate in Gloucestershire. He had three sisters, Mary Frances (Minnie), Sarah Adelaide, who died in 1851, and Letitia Jane Dorothea (Dora). On 28 July 1881, Dora married Richard Baxter Townshend—son of a Londonderry clergyman—and fourteen years later Minnie became the second wife of the Rector of Wolverhampton. All these people are remembered because of their friendship with Alice Robert's husband. Beneath a weathered stone in Hasfield churchyard, around which in spring the primroses cluster and above which is the kind of "remote peace" of which Elgar once wrote, lie the remains of "W. M. B." of the "Enigma" Variations.

At Newland, in the Forest of Dean, Oak House was a very frequent calling-point. There lived Alice's Aunt Caroline, wife of Captain John Henry Dighton. At Dymock, in a house named Hill Ash, "Cousin Vee"—Veronica, sister of Captain Dighton and wife of Stanley Napier Raikes, held court. Mrs. Raikes did

The drawingroom of the Elgars' first home, 51 Avonmore Road, West Kensington.
Watercolour by Alice Elgar, August 1890.

AVE MARIA...

Sunday service in the Bavarian Highlands. Nineteenth century Aquatint.

this in spectacular fashion. She was a professional invalid—the customary condition of retreat for well-bred ladies of that age with too little occupation—and greeted all callers reclining on a *chaise longue.* She explained how it was not possible for her to take any part in the management of her household, or of anything else. She had certain obsessions and phobias, and being convinced that money was dirty would not handle coins unless they had been individually washed. Despite all this, Mrs. Raikes maintained an earthly existence for ninety-six years. Her daughter, Vera, was a close friend of Alice, a little envious—it may be suspected—of Alice's intellectual and artistic abilities, and in later time of Alice's husband and daughter too. After her marriage Alice particularly relished visits by those among the Gloucester notables who had been her friends in youth—like Emma Onslow, the Roper Curzons, the Morgan Prices of Tibberton, and Clementina Maxwell, whose home was in Scotland but was frequently in Gloucestershire.

During the winter season there were balls in the great houses, for which Alice made her own dresses, and there were concerts in the schoolrooms of Gloucestershire and Worcestershire. In the villages Alice was recognised as one possessed of special attributes. She could sing a part in a glee, and she was a steady and reliable accompanist. Her brother Fred was also something of a musician, and when on leave from India and in captain's uniform he cut a dashing figure as he delivered the message of a small number of highly favoured patriotic songs in a stirring tenor. The programme of one concert, given in the Pendock School Room on 29 December 1868, survives.

Alice and Fred provided half of the forces required for the execution of "Come let us be merry", a glee by the local and celebrated composer Robert Lucas Pearsall. The programme contained other glees, by Bishop, Knyvett, and Hime. Captain Roberts—to his sister's accompaniment—sang Benedict's "England yet" and Gray's "Rhein [*sic*] wine". It was, however, in piano duet arrangements of Hérold's *Zampa* and Rossini's *Guillame Tell* overtures that Alice showed her real flair and mastery. Her partner was the accomplished Hyacinth, daughter of Rev. W. S. Symonds, Rector of Pendock.

CONCERT,

AT

PENDOCK SCHOOL ROOM,

December 29th, 1868.

PROGRAMME.—FIRST PART.

GLEE............"Come let us be merry"............PEARSALL.
Mrs Ashfield Miss ROBERTS, MISS SYMONDS, CAPT. ROBERTS, ~~REV. A. FOWLER.~~ Mr Jones

SONG.............."Home, Sweet Home"..............
MRS. HOLMES.

SOLO—VIOLONCELLO..."Murmures du Rhone" ..BURGMULLER.
& piano Miss Symonds
MR. REGINALD SYMONDS.

SONG..........."The Queen of the May"......MRS. ARKWRIGHT.
MRS. ASHFIELD.

SONG.................."England yet"..............BENEDICT.
CAPTAIN ROBERTS.

DUETT—PIANOFORTE.."Zampa"....................HEROLD.
MISS ROBERTS, MISS SYMONDS.

SONG.................."Katey's Letter" ......LADY DUFFERIN.
MISS BARTON.

SONG..........."I watch for thee in starless night"........
MR. BRAND.

SONG................"I love to sing"....................HIME
MRS. J. CLARK.

GLEE........"Where art thou Beam of Light?" ....BISHOP
Miss Roberts MRS. ASHFIELD, MISS SYMONDS. CAPTAIN ROBERTS, ~~REV. A. FOWLER.~~ Jones

SECOND PART.

GLEE......"The bells of Saint Michael's Tower"......KNYVETT
MISS BARTON, MISS SYMONDS, MR. DAVIS.

SONG................"Auld Robin Gray"..............LEEVES
MRS. ASHFIELD.

SONG.............Village "~~King~~ Christmas" Blacksmith..........HATTON
~~REV. A. FOWLER.~~ Mr Jones

DUETT—PIANOFORTE.."Guillaume Tell" ....ROSSINI
MISS ROBERTS, MISS SYMONDS.

SONG.................."The Fairy's Well"..............
& piano Miss Symonds REV. A. WOOD.

SOLO—VIOLONCELLO.."Nocturne"............BURGMULLER
MR. REGINALD SYMONDS.

SONG.................."Rhein wine"...................GRAY
CAPTAIN ROBERTS.

DUET......................"Sol Fa".......................
MRS. ASHFIELD MR. BRAND

SONG.............. "Old Christmas"...............WESTROP
MRS. HOLMES.

GLEE........"I see them on their winding way" ....HIME
Miss Roberts MRS. ASHFIELD, MISS SYMONDS, CAPTAIN ROBERTS, ~~REV. A. FOWLER.~~ Mr J

SONG................"The Whistlin Thief"....................
MR. BRAND.

GOD SAVE THE QUEEN.

Tutti

3
Records of the Rocks

The name of Symonds was one which commanded respect in the country of the Marches. William Symonds, Lord of the Manor of Elsdon, Herefordshire, a sturdy country gentleman, a Justice of the Peace and Deputy Lieutenant for the county married Mary Anne, daughter of Samuel Beale of Upton-on-Severn, who was the patron of the parish of Pendock. Of their children it was William Samuel, the eldest son, who did most to perpetuate the name. Educated in a Cheltenham school, by a private tutor, and at Christ's College, Cambridge, he was ordained deacon in 1841—he was then twenty-four—and priest in 1842 when he was licensed to a curacy at Offenham in the diocese of Worcester. In 1845 he became both Patron of the living and Rector of Pendock. This appointment he held until his death, on 15th September 1887. Having inherited it through his grandfather's trustees he became Lord of the Manor of Pendock. He was also a Justice of the Peace. Pendock church, from the twelfth century, is on a promontory of pasture overlooking a motorway, and its only access is through the fields.

In 1840, Symonds married Hyacinth Catherine, eldest daughter of Samuel Kent, also of Upton-on-Severn. In 1842 a daughter, named Hyacinth, and three years later a son, Powell, were born. The latter grew up to become an officer in the 16th Regiment, but he died in 1879. Another son, Elsdon Henry, died aged seven in 1857 and was buried in Pendock churchyard. Yet another male child, Henry Francis, born in 1855, did not survive infancy. The life of a Victorian family was punctuated by funerals. Hyacinth's father died in 1847, and on 5 November 1859 Rev. H. Taylor conducted the last rites for Symonds's mother, in the churchyard at Pendock where, in 1864, his mother-in-law, Katherine Kent—who had lately been resident in Paris—was also laid to rest.

Symonds, was a purposeful individual, one with a considerable sense of public duty, and a polymath. To the people of Pendock and the surrounding districts he knew everything. And he was willing to offer himself to a wider public as an authority on a number of things. Fortunately he did not fall victim to the malady which led so many of his contemporaries in his profession to publish sermons. He was essentially interested in geology, and what he wrote on this science was based on much work in the field.

When he was a curate at Offenham, near Evesham, Symonds became friendly with Hugh Edwin Strickland (1811–53), of Apperley, in Gloucestershire. A considerable authority on geology, Strickland was largely responsible for the rules of zoological nomenclature adopted by the British Association in 1842. These rules were reprinted in 1863 by Sir William Jardine, whose widowed daughter Catherine Dorcas married Strickland in 1845. In 1845 the Cotteswold Naturalists' Field Club—one of the earliest of such clubs in England—was founded at the Black Horse, Birdlip. This was altogether a memorable year, for Strickland's honeymoon tour led him through Saxony and the museums in Berlin, Leipzig, and Dresden—from where he and his bride wandered happily in the Saxon Switerland above the Elbe.

Young Symonds took note of all that he heard and read, and the results of his studies were not slow to follow.[1] He was for ever conducting groups of young and eager enthusiasts into the western hills, where he discoursed not only on nature but also the fragilities of man. Concerning the latter he assembled his ideas particularly in two historical novels—the one concerning

[1] Symonds made a number of references to Strickland in *Records of the Rocks*, of which the first is particularly charming:

> It was on the summit of the "Ragged Stone" that, in 1853, Mr. Hugh Strickland, then Reader in Geology at Oxford, gave his last lecture to an assemblage of naturalists, who gathered around its peak to listen to one who was ever ready with a kind word, and courteous hand. Now, "when the setting sun lights up the peaks of the 'Ragged Stone', it shines full upon the obituary window erected to his memory in the old church of Deerhurst, in the Severn Vale, and those last rays play upon the words, 'To the memory of Hugh Edwin Strickland, the tribute of many friends' " (pp. 35–6)

the Wars of the Roses and the other the Civil Wars of the seventeenth century, and their effect on the life of the region.

In 1853 Symonds was elected to membership of the Cotteswold Club. Soon afterwards he founded the Malvern Naturalists' Field Club and was its President until 1871. He was also a member of the sister Clubs of Worcester and Woolhope. In 1874 he took time off from his parish commitments to visit geological formations in Auvergne and Ardèche. Three years later his health began to give cause for concern and in 1883 he went down south to live with his daughter and son-in-law.

Symonds twice contributed papers to the *Edinburgh New Philosophical Journal*, on "Geology as it affects Plurality of Worlds", in 1855–6, and "On the Geology of the railway from Worcester to Hereford" in 1861–2. In 1863 he published his "Address on the enjoyment to be derived from the study of Natural Science", in 1864 "Notes on a Ramble through North Wales", which had started life as a lecture to the Worcester Natural History Society, and in 1869 a lecture of which the subject was "Progress and Development". In the popular field he wrote *Old Bones*, a study of fossils "for young naturalists" and *Old Stones*, about the rocks near Malvern, for the same audience, and both books ran into three editions. His masterpiece, however, was *Records of the Rocks*.

At this point we return to Hyacinth Symonds, Alice Roberts's piano duet partner and one of the firmest friends of her formative years. Hyacinth was an attractive example to Alice in that she showed how by marriage it was possible for the intelligent girl to escape from the inhibitions imposed by conventional inward-looking, parochial attitudes.

Hyacinth made not one interesting marriage, but, because the partner of the first did not long survive what for him was a second union contracted late in life, two. Both marriages derived from her father's insatiable thirst for scientific knowledge, and the hospitality he was able to offer to men of distinction.

Sir William Jardine (1800–74), Scottish naturalist, ornithologist, and sometime Commissioner for Salmon Fisheries, was one of Symond's acquaintances through the Strickland association. The consequence of his visiting Pendock is to be read in the Parish Register in this form:

1871, 18 November; Marriage Solemnised at Pendock in the Parish of Pendock in the County of Worcester.
William Jardine full age widower Baronet of Applegirth [Father] Alexander Jardine [Rank or Profession of father] Baronet. Hyacinth Symonds full age spinster . . .

The marriage was solemnised by the bride's father and in post-nuptial shock Hyacinth signed herself as Hyacinth (Jardine, deleted) Symonds. Three years later she was a widow, from which state, however, she was rescued by another scientific friend of her father.

Sir Joseph Hooker (1817–1911) was not only one of the great scientists of his day, but also a man of many parts. He was a friend of Alexander von Humboldt on the one hand and of Charles Darwin on the other. His first wife, Frances, was a daughter of Professor Henslow, the Cambridge botanist who had recommended Darwin for the post of naturalist on the famous exploration of the Beagle in 1831. Hooker was also friendly with Charles Kingsley. In 1839 he sailed away to the Antarctic and subsequently published his findings in *Antarctica Flora* (1843–60)—which was a subject of subsequent inspiration for Alice Roberts. After explorations in India, Hooker published his *Himalayan Journals* in 1854. Yet none of this precluded friendship with the Rector of Pendock, and after the death of William Jardine in 1874, and of Frances, his wife, two years later, it seemed eminently sensible to marry Hyacinth Jardine. After their wedding they spent some part of their honeymoon in North Wales, and a year later the first of two sons, Joseph Symonds Hooker, was born. It was characteristic of Hooker—an intrepid character—that he should at this point go on a scientific expedition to the Rocky Mountains and into California. In the same year of 1877 he was knighted in the Order of the Star of India, a proper prelude to an Indian summer and introduction to the good graces of the Roberts's.

Hooker was an attractive man. He loved children and was known to play at being an Old Lion for his son Joseph—the Young Lion, and this playful relationship is documented in his extant letters. He was a collector of Wedgwood ware (a medallion in his honour was issued by the firm) and a lover of Handel's music. A hater of theological dogmatism, he could not "understand the Church ignoring the teaching of the Buddhists", and was prominent in his support of liberalising tendencies in the Church of England. His father-in-law at Pendock, also promoting liberalism, was a congenial companion and in his last years Symonds lived with the Hookers at the house, The Camp, which they built at Sunningdale.

Sir Joseph Hooker included among his duties at one time or another the Directorship of the Royal Gardens at Kew and the Presidency of the Royal Society. He was vigorous to the end of his life, and when over ninety years of age played his part in the Darwin Centenary Celebrations at Cambridge.[2]

A third famous guest at Pendock in the days when Alice was a constant visitor was Sir Charles Lyell (1797–1875), a lawyer, geologist, Professor of Geology in King's College, London in 1831, and President of the British Association in 1864. Lyell was a fine classical scholar, a lover of poetry, strongly liberal in outlook, and a close friend of Kingsley. In 1864 he submitted his views on the structure of education to the Public Schools Commission. In supporting Faraday's contention that scientific training should have an assured place in education he thought "the literary writings of a man like Hallam, for instance, who had taught himself science and natural history, are of a higher stamp than they would have been if he had not had that knowledge". He further opined that the clergy would benefit for acquiring scientific knowledge, feeling that there was at that time "a dangerous want of sympathy between the better informed working-classes of the manufacturing districts and the clergy".[3] In respect of clerical affairs, Lyell had the example of Symonds before him, so too had Alice Roberts, surely the most

[2] Hyacinth's mother died at the beginning of 1907, aged 88, and was buried at Pendock on 14 January; Hyacinth herself, described incorrectly in the Parish Register as "wife of Sir Hooker founded Kew Garden", died at Littleridge, Pendock, where she lived as a châtelaine, and was buried on 13 December 1921.

[3] *Chambers's Journal*, 1864, p. 661
As he quoted from Strickland and Hooker, so did Symonds cite Lyell in the work which would not have come into being except for Lyell's example and research.

devoted of all Symonds's pupils and his frequent companion on his excursions.

There is a letter (from the summer of 1871) from Symonds to Alice indicating the seriousness with which the pupil treated her geological studies. She was, indeed, not only following the master but also (as will be shown in more detail on p. 58) her own creative star.

My dear Alice

I send you by post today some notes *wh* should precede your Volcanic & Earthquake chapter viz, on the evidences of a beginning.

The 'Records of a Hammer' by an Old Chisel will not be a bad title & then I can say a thing or two under the nom de plume I should hardly care to say as *Revd. W. S. S.!* Please try and suppose *you* have been my *fellow rambler* and don't hesitate to draw upon *your imagination*. I will keep the 'Records' *scientifically* correct & that is all we want.

Soar into the clouds with the Spectrum, and dive into the recesses of the earth with the mining tool! ! Please come on Sunday!

Mr. Scobell has obtained leave to open Mr. Bannerman's cave so I go down there to set them going next week, perhaps. Mrs. Scobell has collected some funds. I have now before me the proofs of the Edin^{r} papers for the Geol Magz for October.[4] Send me a line to Sir W. Guise's Elmore Court, Gloster where I go tomorrow for two or three days.

Yours ever sincerely,
W. S. Symonds.

Symonds had long hoped that the caves of the Great Doward in the Wye Valley might be explored, since what he had found in the cavern known as King Arthur's Cave led him to suppose that there were many finds of geological significance to be made. In the summer of 1870 some miners working iron ore uncovered fossil bones. A Mr. Fryer, of Coleford, forwarded to Symonds, a "tooth of fossil horse". Shortly afterwards, Sir James Campbell, "Gaveller of Dean Forest", visited the site and sent specimens to London. Excited by this, Symonds obtained permission from Sir James Campbell to proceed with further exploration. Supported by a grant from the Malvern Field Club,

[4] *The Geological Magazine*, LXXXVIII, Oct. 1871, pp. 433–8.

Jem the Slipper.

fortified by professional opinions from Professor Richard Owen (1804–92), and Messrs. William Boyd Dawkins (1837–1929) and John Evans (1823–1908), celebrated palaeontologists, and assisted on the site by Mr. Scobell of Doward House and "the well-known cave dweller of modern days, 'Jem the Slipper' ", who lived in the Great Doward, he made many discoveries. In August 1870 he notified the discovery of relics of "Mammoth, Rhinoceros, and Horse" to the British Association Meeting in Liverpool. In the following year he read a paper, "On the contents of a Hyaena's Den on Great Doward, Whitchurch, Ross" at the Edinburgh Conference of the B.A. In due course this was discussed in the work by which Symonds became best known.

In 1872 the reputable publishing house of John Murray, of Albemarle Street, issued *Records of the Rocks or Notes on the Geology, Natural History and, Antiquities of North & South Wales, Devon & Cornwall*, by Rev. W. S. Symonds, Fellow of the Geographic Society. This was the crowning achievement of Symonds's career, and one of those contributions to culture which for so long provided justification for the freedom allowed to the clergy of the Church of England. Symonds's interests remind us that he was a contemporary with Charles Kingsley, with whom—if he did not—his son-in-law maintained contact. Like Kingsley he sought through science to discover new means by which to explain to man some of the ways of God.

Symonds made no excessive claims for his book. It was by an amateur, for amateurs, "who, like myself, enjoy passing their leisure hours among Rocks, old Castles, old Authors, and the wild flowers of strange wayside places". What was intended as a geological survey in fact becomes a repository for philosophic ideas of a more or less general nature, linked together by respect for the authority of history, or accepted moral law, and appreciation of natural environment. *Records of the Rocks* is both a tour of the countryside, and of a well-stocked library. And Symonds was no mean stylist. He could capture atmosphere and contain it in free-flowing prose.

> When last we were on the summit of Queenaig, it was on an evening in October; the sun was setting brightly, a golden eagle floated in the air above our heads, while the snowfinch flickering

past gave warning of an approaching winter. Canisp and Suilven stood out like the Egyptian pyramids, to which Hugh Miller likened them, and one, who had examined their history, felt certain that their strata had been once continuous, stretching from peak to peak; that they had then been eroded, and cut out by ice, for high up, on all, are the striae and scratches of that powerful agent which once had so great an influence in moulding the hills and vales of Scotland.[5]

Scientific explanation of this kind was a delightful and decorous pastime, with opportunity for indulging in a sport that was conveniently related.

Only this summer I assisted some friends in capturing the Alpine char (Salmo salvelinus), from a small rock basin on the east side of Ben Hope in Sutherlandshire; and here, side by side with the fish, was the cloudberry (Rubus chamaemorus) and Saxifraga aizoides growing profusely on the banks of the lake, 2000 feet above the sea.[6]

Legends were picked up, neatly laid out and dressed with a tolerant scepticism.

At St. Harman's near Rhayader, in mid-Wales, was said to have been

a staff of St. Cyric, which was especially efficacious in the removal of glandular swellings, if "devout application of the staff were made", "with the oblation of one penny". The staff, however, was somewhat particular about receiving its due tribute.

As it happened in the days of Giraldus that a patient presenting a halfpenny the disease subsided only in the middle; and another coming with the promise of a penny was cured, but failing to fulfil his engagement, his sufferings returned, and he had to pay threepence to obtain a cure.[7]

Symonds examined the history of coal in detail and with a recognition of Paley's lasting influence, some part of his introduction to this theme reaches even beyond the present day.

Coal is now so intimately associated with the future destinies of Great Britain as well as with our idea of comfort and enjoyment, that it is not surprising if some of us believe that there is something in the history of its composition, storing, and preservation . . .

[5] *Records of the Rocks*, pp. 24–5.
[6] *ibid.*, pp. 108–9.
[7] *ibid.*, pp. 134–5.

which must be referred to a scheme of Providence and Design rather than to a blind collection of vegetable matter which grew by chance, was accumulated by chance, and was turned into coal by chance....

... The importance of coal in a national point of view can only be estimated by reflecting on what would become of Great Britain without the agent which warms our hearths, heats our forges, smelts our metals, illumines by its gases at night our cities, streets, and dwelling-houses, propels our locomotive engines and carries thousands of steam vessels, often against the storm wind, over the most distant seas.[8]

Not far from Redmarley was the Forest of Dean, where

the coals are being worked on their outcrop; and the pits are entered by horizontal tunnels. The Coal-measures are wretched botanising ground and famous principally for *Nettles*. The poorer miners still use nettles as an ingredient in spring salads and for nettle broth.[9]

Beyond that point were problems which the author did not examine quite closely. God's purposes were sometimes inscrutable, even to a man of science.

Records of the Rocks was given a flattering five-page review in the January 1873 issue of *The Geological Magazine*. It was, it was said, "the work of a master upon the subject". It is certainly a companionable volume. It was dedicated to Sir Charles Lyell in acknowledgement of the debt owed by the author to that master of the subject. In addition to reproduction of illustrations from Sir Roderick Murchison's *Siluria*,[10] the book contains a large number of quite charming scenic sketches by Sir William F. L. S. Guise,[11] and a number of drawings of fossils

[8] *ibid.*, pp. 367–9.

[9] *ibid.*, pp. 388–9.

[10] Sir Roderick Impey Murchison (1792–1871) soldier until 1814, became interested in science, a friend of Sir Humphry Davy, and a specialist in the study of old red sandstone, to which he assigned the name Silurian. He published his *The Silurian System* in 1838. From 1843 to 1858 Murchison was President of the Royal Geographical Society, and from 1855 to 1871 Director-General of the Geological Survey.

[11] Guise succeeded T. B. Lloyd Baker, the first to hold the office, as President of the Cotteswold Naturalists' Field Club in 1859. He remained in office until 1886. It was said that "to become a member it was necessary to prove acceptable to him personally." At the family seat at Elmore Court, near Gloucester, were paintings by Velasquez, Murillo, Lely, Reynolds, Gainsborough and others.

by Dorothea Baker. The last word in the Preface is reserved for "Miss Roberts, of Hazeldine, Red Marley, for efficient aid in carrying the MSS through the press, and for the copious Index."

In this literally down to earth manner Alice began her career in the world of letters. Having seen the completion of his *magnum opus* Symonds began to think of his duty towards his lieutenants. He wrote to Alice as follows:

42 Regents Park Road
Thursday 28 Nov. [1872]

My dear Alice
I went to the Junr Army and Navy Club yesterday *as soon as possible* after I arrived in Town but your Brother was out and they could not tell me where his lodgings were [;] so write me word by return—However I left *my* address—

I ordered too yesterday two books [—] one the last edition of Sir C. Lyell's 'Students [Student's] Elements [of Geology, 1871]', and the other my last edition [1864] of 'Old Bones' and directed them to be sent to Hazeldine as some little token that I really do appreciate your great kindness in helping me to arrange and recopy, and readjust my 'Records'—I hope both books may be useful my dear friend in other days and perhaps when you may be rambling or journeying away from the glades of Red Marley and the hills of the Malverns.

I heard from Sir W. Jardine yesterday morning—They are well and happy he says and so he *ought to be* with his young bride and loved one—They go to Lyme Regis this week I suppose [.] I find my friends here have filled up every day with engagements up to Saturday before I arrived but if your Brother is able to go I shall take him about in the day time—

Do you know I drove home round by Red Marley on Saturday as I was told I should meet Lady Roberts & you going to Hasfield [Court, home of the Bakers] but I saw you not & I could not go on to Hazeldine as I had to write letters on business for the post. My kindest regards to Lady Roberts.

Your sincere friend
W. S. Symonds

Alice's presentation copy of *Records of the Rocks* "from her sincere friend" was dated 13 December 1872.

Although Alice would seem to have been compiling notes towards an exercise of her own it was not until after the appearance of *Records of the Rocks* that she set down a title page:

Worlds from my Window
a
Geological Essay
by
C.A.R.

(Miss C. A. Roberts
Hazeldine
Redmarley
Newent
Gloucestershire)

If Alice showed no great sense of scientific originality she demonstrated correctness in scholarly practice by identifying her sources, of which the main ones were her master's *Records of the Rocks* and *Stones of the Valley* (1875), Lyell's classic *Principles of geology* (1830),[12] *Elements of geology* (1838) and *Student's Elements of geology* (a gift from Symonds), David Page's (1814–79) *Introductory Textbook of geology* (1854)[13] and Murchison's *Outline of the geology of the neighbourhood of Cheltenham* (1834).[14]

It is not, however, the student scientist who compels attention, but the imaginative process by which this girl could interpret what she saw. The opening of her Essay runs as follows:

> My window commands a view of a large tract of country stretching away towards the far blue horizon. The worlds I see from it exhibit not the busy stir of a populous town, neither the ceaseless labour and gloomy chimnies [*sic*] of mines and factories, nor the more healthful activity of a sea-side port or fishing town. Nothing of this kind can be seen from my window, but, in their place, lies a broad expanse of inland scenery, varied only by the undulations of hill and valley, cultivated fields and green woods. The worlds I would speak of then, are the worlds which have long since passed away, but the history of which, thanks to the labours of men of science, has gradually been brought to light. . . .
> . . . We cannot claim for it the grandeur of lofty mountains, the majesty of primeval forests of the lordliness of mighty rivers, but

[12] This work once ranked second only to Darwin's *Origin of Species*, the author of which—a close friend of Lyell—once said, "I always feel as if my books came half out of Lyell's brain". The Natural History Museum, London, organised a centenary exhibition devoted to Lyell in the summer of 1975.

[13] This ran into many editions, the tenth appearing in 1873.

[14] A new edition, revised and enlarged by J. Buchman and H. E. Strickland, was issued in 1845.

the scene before us has many charms peculiar to itself. The grassy slopes glitter in the summer sun, hills rise in picturesque chains, or stand isolated, and covered with woods, old timbered farmhouses, once stately manors, can be discerned, & the smoke from cottages, half buried amongst the foliage of the coppices, curls tranquilly above them, such is the world of today.

The world as seen then in the 1870's, she goes on, was not what had been seen by previous eyes, nor would it always remain as it seemed. Yet it was a beautiful world, and even when considering change in structure one should look on it with a sense of its enchantment. Alice makes it clear that the ultimate responsibility for the nature of the world was with God. Yet she can pick up a hint of other and malign authorities in the supernatural; her access to them was through the folk philosophies current in Redmarley.

From the present she proceeds to the distant past, and the curtain goes up on the most familiar features of her immediate environment:

One of the most marked features is a chain of hills, the Malvern range, which extends for about twelve miles in a northerly direction—They rise somewhat suddenly and abruptly, and although they attain no very great height, they are extremely picturesque and bold in outline, the flatness of the plain on the eastern side probably adding considerably to their apparent size and eminence—Beautiful are they to look on whether clear and bright in the sunshine, or when, enveloped in the wintry mists, they can only be seen in vague shadowy outlines—They are too most varied in form; the first and nearest is low and rounded, behind it rises a higher double peaked hill. Its eastern point is sharp in contour, and even now, a lingering tradition amongst the peasants causes them to dread its shadow resting on them or their dwellings. A little to the west stands a hill which is easily recognised as the site of an ancient encampment, and so the line stretches on now in long ridges, now rising in sharp peaks. The sheep browse tranquilly on the grassy slopes, towns and villages have sprung up nestling against their flanks, but at the commencement of the great period, the earliest known to geologists, they wore a far different aspect. For these hills are believed to belong to the most ancient of all geological formations, the Laurentian, strata which are largely developed in Canada and the United States of America, but which in Great Britain, occur only in the Hebrides, the Northern countries of Scotland, in a few isolated patches in Wales and in these Worcestershire hills. . . .

At the end of her story she slowly brings the curtain down:

> Let us now close my window, the shadows are deepening into twilight and the ancient worlds sink again into the night of darkness from whence we called them for awhile. . . .

Alice laid aside her pen. A neat pile of revised blue foolscap sheets, covered with the bold, sloping, writing lay before her. Whatever the burdens laid on her by Roberts's, Raikes's, Probyns and the "peasants" of Redmarley, Lowbands and Pendock, and the fashionable coteries of Cheltenham and Malvern, she had her own secret world.

4
World of Letters

Alice's alert sense of curiosity, disposition to seek for first causes, awareness of the innate creativity of human beings, and a streak of radicalism in her make-up that led her to question the doctrine of the inferiority of women—largely subscribed to by most women of her kind and generation—all led her in her own quiet way to kick over the traces. This exercise was according to the time-honoured method available to her sex. She committed her thoughts and views to writing. Her observations on geological formations and natural history took her to the edge of imaginative speculation; but she wished to go further than this. Her frustrations—and the older she grew the more they became—turned her towards poetry and fiction, in some cases the two became one.

When Alice was helping Symonds she was an eager girl in her early twenties. She was small, with blue eyes, and fair hair that darkened somewhat as she grew older, but even at the end of her life showed little grey. In Redmarley D'Abitot she was properly classed as an intellectual, not least of all when in 1882 her most celebrated work—*Marchcroft Manor*, a novel in two volumes—was published. By now she was past thirty, and her widowed mother was still hale and hearty. Alice by this time must have been supposed to have passed beyond the limits of marriageable probability—and profitability—and to have taken her place among those unfortunates whose fate it was, immured in involuntary celibacy, to pass through a generation as a tiresome aunt or godmother. Stanley Napier was married and on 26 May 1879 his daughter, Theodora, was born, to whose welfare Alice could well dedicate herself in a patronal capacity. She had, however, set herself on an alternative course.

In her writings, inasmuch as they have survived, we have a record of Alice's spiritual development. She wrote short stories for children; lyric and narrative poems; translations from German and Italian; and novels. Among her earliest extant pieces are *The Snowflake* (1877?), a flimsy piece released by reflection on some lines of Tennyson, and *Family Pride*, a morality after Aesop and Sarah Trimmer (who, through her interest in Sunday Schools had an oblique relationship with the Raikes's), dated 11 November 1877. From this point Alice looked forward to becoming a writer of children's books—like Mary Butt maybe. The celebrated author of *The History of the Fairchild Family* was a native of Worcestershire, who had lived in India for some time after her marriage to an officer in the Indian Army. There was also the stimulation of Charles Kingsley, whose *Water Babies* (cf. Alice's *Down, down, down,/Down to the depths of the sea*) was published in 1863, and who was personally known to the Symonds family, and of Charles Dodgson (Lewis Carroll), whose *Alice in Wonderland* appeared two years after Kingsley's classic. *Through the looking glass* was issued in 1872, the same year as *Records of the Rocks*. There is an echo of Dodgson in a curious tale, *Marian's Party*, on which Alice put no date.

> Marian thought she would make haste and go to sleep, but on opening her eyes for a moment she saw such a strange party assembled in the room that she sat up to see who all the people could be. . . .
>
> There were many figures, men and women, and they were all in black and at first Marian thought it must be a funeral party till she saw that they danced quite merrily on the wall, and heard them laughing and talking so she thought it must be the latest fashion to dress in black.

The characters in this fantasy were as from the worlds of Jonson or Bunyan—Miss de High Life, Lord Made of Money, Lady Sweet-help—and so on. *Human Life*, another undated morality of the same period, promotes its serious intention through Goethe's

> Seele des Menschen
> Wie gleichst du dem Wasser!

The story, such as it is, is related by a water-lily, Germanly meditating on the vanity of human wishes.

Some of Alice's poems in respect of imagery relate to her stories. The "snow" concept, for example, carries right through from the early observations from her window at Hazeldine into the music of Edward Elgar. On 29 December 1877, she wrote a piece "For a Child", entitled *The Snow:*

> Oh snow which sinks so light,
> Brown earth is hid from sight.
> O soul be thou as white
> As the snow, as the snow.

This was completed at nine o'clock in the morning Alice noted, and was the climax of a three day sojourn with inspiration. On 27 December she had written *Autumn*. On the next day she finished *The Reply*, a gloomy contemplation of human misery a long way after Clough. In 1890 Alice looked back at this piece and inscribed a gloss: "I trust a happier faith now. C.A.E." This was after a year of marriage. As for *The Snow*, slightly revised, that passed into *Isabel Trevithoe* and thence into Elgar's music.

In 1878 Alice was feverishly busy with her pen. Like many of her generation she was deferential to the past. The illusion of a former age of gold persisted and it grew more obsessive as it merged into her later adoration of her husband's music which was to seem—at least unconsciously—a fulfilment of her own aspirations as a creative artist. In April Alice wrote a poem about [*The Battle* of] *Senlac* (Hastings); in July, as a follow-up to an article by Sidney Colvin in the April issue of the *New Quarterly Magazine*,[1] *The Fight for the Shrine*; in August a soliloquy on the word *Miserrimus* standing singly on a tomb in Worcester Cathedral;[2] and (also in August) a romantic fantasia

[1] Colvin's article "The Apollo Belvedere" (pp. 31–46), is a demolition of Winckelmann's argument that the sculpture in question, at Delphi, was a masterpiece. To Colvin it was theatrical and decadent. Alice, writing a polemic against French archaeologists' disregard of the decencies of archaeological practice, disagrees with Colvin.

[2] ". . . The little flat stone on the pavement of the north-west cloister inscribed with the thrilling word "Miserrimus". It has been stated that this stone covers the remains of the Rev. Thomas Morris, or Maurice, who, at the Revolution, refusing to acknowledge the King's supremacy was deprived of his preferment, depended for the rest of his life on the benevolence of various Jacobites; & that at his death he requested that the only inscription on his grave might be "Miserrimus!" Wordsworth has written some pathetic lines on this subject". *Littlebury's Guide to Worcester and its Neighbourhood*. 3rd edition, 1883, p. 28.

on an account given by Cousin Vee of a visit to "a castle on the North coast of Ireland"—presumably Dunluce. This seascape is a companion piece to one of 11 November 1879, *To the Sea at Porth-kernow* (Porthcurnow), prompted, no doubt, by Roden Noel's "Rambles by Cornish Seas" in *Macmillan's Magazine*, 1876[3] (Roden Noel figures in the catalogue of Elgar's works as the author of the "Sea Slumber Song" in *Sea Pictures*.)

In these pieces, intended to furnish Hazeldine with additional cultural memorials, Alice somewhat extended the view from her window. She wrote for the most part with amiability and a mechanical competence. But occasionally one is less aware of derivativeness than of the suggestion of later voices. This, for instance could pass across the county boundaries into Housman country:

Swift roll the years and shadows fly,
The sunbeams gleam, we laugh and sigh,
Now joy may dawn, now fast decline,
But one sad memory is thine.
Miserrimus.

There are some poems of this period in which the cry *Miserrimus* turns inward. On 6 November 1878 Alice addressed four stanzas *To* ———:

Thou lullest thy soul as with sighs of the deep
'Mongst shadows the vainest, the sweetest to sleep,
Midst visions soft-cradled of measureless bliss
Only roused the sweet pain by a dream-covered kiss.

Some years later Alice salvaged a set of 1878 poems—*Songs of the Seasons and Hope*—and recopied them, adding the inscription "For E. E. from C. A. E." This was after some part of that dream had come true.

On 14 April 1879, in *Désillusionné* she wrote

. . . I find a chilling blank, where fades
My dream of life and withers in my hand.

Two days later came *Telle est la vie—quelquefois*

And that is past and that
And what yet may remain?

[3] XXXIV, pp. 334–41.

Dim burning eyes
Slow sobs that rise
No more than that.

The echoes of Pre-Raphaelitism here heard are caught up in a more consciously derived tribute to this school.

In May 1880, Alice went to London to see the Summer Exhibition at the Grosvenor Gallery. The most imposing picture that year was Sydney P. Hall's *Chapter of the Order of the Star of India held at Calcutta, January 1st 1876; H.R.H. the Prince of Wales investing the Maharaja of Jodpoor.* Also shown in that picture was Alice's kinsman Dighton Macnaughten Probyn (son of Capt. George Probyn), who had won the V.C. at Agra after the capture of Delhi in 1857, and who was now a Major-General and Comptroller and Treasurer to the Household of the Prince of Wales. (Dighton became yet another of the family's nonagenarians. Born in 1833 he died in 1924.) At the Exhibition Alice also had the chance, by way of contrast, to look at Walter Crane's delicate water-colours. But for her the real eye-catcher was No. 120 in the East Gallery, Burne-Jones's *The Golden Stairs*, described in the Catalogue as:

> a large, upright composition of eighteen minstrels clad in greyish white, descending barefooted a flight of pale, golden stairs. They enter on the left hand from a logia of white marble, passing down the staircase which forms a graceful curve from left to right in the picture. This is one of Mr. Burne-Jones's most characteristic and thoughtful pictures; a sad Mantagnesque. . . .

This was a new picture, and to Alice a real revelation both of earthly and heavenly beauty. She wrote her response in *The Golden Stair* [*sic*] on 1 June. A company of blessed damozels, pure, untouchable, and distinctly not of Redmarley, were poised for ever in an irrefragible serenity:

For nothing earthly do they care
But ever dreaming onward fare,
With pensive, distant air,
Adown the Golden Stair.

Later in that same month she captured melancholy in a piece that contains a throb of the caged passion that was painfully felt beneath the seemingly tranquil surface of life at Redmarley. On 21 June 1880, she looked on the passage of youth, with regret. With whom, we ask, did Alice once walk among the heather?

Yesterday.

We walked afar o'er heathered slope
We spoke full long of life and hope
Bright shone the sun, the air was stirred
With happy sounds of bee and bird.
But yesterday
Is far away.

We walk no more, we talk no more
Each dwells on far divided shore
The hours are dull and life seems told
A dream unreal of years of old.
So far away
Is yesterday.

But years are long and turns the tide
And wanderers seek the old hill side
But years are long and break the spell
That shed a fragrance as it fell
Which to-morrow
May not borrow.

So hasten not to leave the past
Nor beckon years to fly too fast
Nor call on Time's revolving power
To foil to-day and change the hour
For to-morrow
May bring sorrow.

Like *The Wind at Dawn*, written on 15 August, *Yesterday* was published in due course, in *Home Chimes*, I, no. 31, in August 1884. (In the same journal, on 17 May, Alice's short story *Two Summers* had appeared.) That the summer of 1880 was a period of strain is testified by another poem, *Storm or Calm*.

. . . Yet midst the divers, 'wildered paths I tread
Which lead across the world, I mark a face
Sometimes amongst the throng, on which has place
A look of peace. . . .

Oh! would it not be well, I ask thee, heart,
Keen heart, too quickly stirred by every breeze
That drifts across the path of life, to seize

Such height of calm and fence thee well from change.
Keen heart, exulting, rapt, when thou could'st range
Midst kindred souls with aims and strivings meet
Or pass the gladsome hour in converse
While voice responsive wakes a slumbering flame . . .

And lo ! it haps that on some height of joy
This fitful heart, o'erswept by fresh annoy
Is touched to sudden dissonance and though
Late tuned to harmony, down leaps, and low
Sobs out its wail through all a minor mode.

A connection between poetry and life is assured by a later pencil note on the manuscript of this poem which Alice added in August or September 1888. At that critical point of her life she looked again at this poem, and wrote below it: "A true picture of A's self."

Written into Alice's history so far is a tension born of that wish for independence which had begun to show itself publicly in a number of women of her own privileged class. Aspirations for a freer life in her case more than some were hindered by the sense of duty inculcated into members of a military family on the one hand, and the virtuous widowhood of Lady Roberts on the other. The latter was a reflection of the awe-inspiring image of sanctified desolation presented by the Queen. Moreover, if at Redmarley life was less than exciting there was a guarantee of lasting comfort and, in the likely event of perpetual spinsterhood, also of long-term security. Within an unwritten contract there was the understanding that Alice would continue responsive to the whims of her mother, and of the extensive network of Roberts, Raikes, Probyn, and Dighton cousins and aunts.

Redmarley, however, was not all that far away from places where early skirmishes in the war of female liberation took place. Florence Nightingale used to visit Malvern with her Aunt Mai, and Dorothea Beale took charge of, and revolutionised the Ladies' College in Cheltenham, where also she established the first residential college for the training of women teachers in 1885. This was the era in which Girton College and Newnham College were founded in Cambridge, and London University allowed women to submit themselves for degrees.

Alice's academic inclinations—stimulated by Symonds, the

books that came from the London Library, the intellectual climate of the surrounding towns, and visits to London and further afield, found outlet in essays, translations, and poems. She was for ever busy with her pen—increasingly an instrument of compensation as well as for inspiration—and the very range of her literary activities betokens a restlessness of spirit if not, indeed, discontent. It is not altogether surprising that she had a regard for Kingsley—a Symonds figure, but in a more heroic mould—which is symbolised not only by the watery fantasy of some of her fiction but also by quotations from his works at the head of several of her pieces. At the head of her unpublished children's story *He would be a hero* (after 1882) she placed Kingsley's "Do noble things, not dream them all day long". The influence of Kingsley as social reformer is contained in *He would be a hero* at the outset:

> When Richard Lovell was going to school one morning he met a poor little ragged child who looked very thin and hungry. She asked Richard for a half penny, only a half penny, but he had just had a very good breakfast and thought it ridiculous for anyone to be hungry so soon after breakfast time, and ran on with his half penny and another beside it in his pocket. In the middle of the day he thought he should like to spend his penny on a tart, so he and some others ran down to the shop near the school and just at the window looking at all the nice fresh bread and cakes was the same poor beggar child. She looked very piteously at Richard as he went in, but he took no heed; he spent his penny and enjoyed his tart himself and presently went home to a good dinner.

On the Wing, of the Wind: A Night Journey to the Arctic Seas is another moral tale, related perhaps to the early explorations of Joseph Hooker and based on Alice's more specific studies with Symonds. The hero of the story is Dr. Graham, whose collection of fossils and scientific interests suggests that Symonds's friend Dr. Henry (a benefactor to Redmarley Church) was the original for this character study. In the story it is a small boy, Johnny, who is the beneficiary of Dr. Graham's knowledge and sympathy. Johnny was a poor boy, and the condition of the poor is a theme which assumes large proportions in Alice's thinking. If she treats it with a degree of sentimentality presently out of fashion it should be observed that it is better than not to have treated it at all. The sentiment in this instance is at both ends. Johnny is poor. The doctor is a widower, forever turning in his solitude to the portrait of his young, departed-this-life, wife—a familiar Chantrey subject. Dr. Graham

> was a kind man and so good to the poor people in the town. Indeed he hardly ever doctored rich people, he had plenty of money of his own, so he liked to try to help those who had none.

He was not above the occasional homily, so that he told Johnny

> that if he loved to be out in the sunshine and watch the flowers, and the insects, and search for fossils, and if he could enjoy reading about them in the house, he would never find the time dull and heavy, and would grow up a much nobler and better man.

This story was prefaced by a quatrain from Adelaide Ann Proctor, for whom Alice had a considerable respect. Whatever her qualities as a poet Mrs. Proctor also deserves commemoration for her concern for women's rights, a matter which also aroused the concern of Kingsley and his friend and mentor F. D. Maurice. The trend towards female emancipation was almost entirely the result of severe middle class frustration and concern, and there was a fair chance that it would remain a middle class interest. The "condition of the poor" was in general treated as a separate issue, but there were those who saw that discrimination was indivisible. Among these the most notable figures were Octavia Hill (1838–1912), a disciple of F. D. Maurice and also of John Ruskin, and Angela Burdett-Coutts. Baroness Burdett-Coutts touched Alice's world directly, for, a geological enthusiast too, she was a friend of Sir Joseph Hooker.

Both Octavia Hill and Angela Burdett-Coutts were pioneers in the reformation of attitude towards housing, and in this field their achievements were comparable to those of Florence Nightingale in other sectors of public health. Baroness Burdett-Coutts—one of the most remarkable women of her own or any other time—was active in every department of social welfare in the widest sense. She had a genius for seeing problems as interrelated and for searching for total solutions. So model housing in Bethnal Green brought in the general welfare of children and "young persons", the reorganisation of the food trade in the interest of the consumer, adequate provision for the stabling of costermongers' horses, the alleviation of unemployment through emigration. She helped to found the NSPCC, after having worked with the Ragged School Union. She established youth clubs and in 1879 organised a Flower Girls' Brigade for the benefit of all Eliza Doolittles.

Alice Roberts was not an activist in the manner of Burdett-Coutts, or of her own cousin Emily (see p. 26), but more than most of her acquaintances it would seem that she not only saw that changes in the structure of society were imminent but also that they were necessary. That there should have been a tincture of radicalism in her make-up should not be altogether surprising; she was, after all, the great-granddaughter of Robert Raikes. In *The Portrait*, a long short story, and in *Isabel Trevithoe*, written two years later, the theme of the young woman of gentle birth distinguishing herself by a concern for intellectual and social issues, is quite extensively developed. In *Marchcroft Manor*, the ambitious two-volume novel of 1882, the dominant interest is in the exposition of a radical view-point.

In each of these works may be discovered Alice's ideal husband: a grave intellectual—in two cases a barrister—of advancing years, with a strong feeling for social justice, and a considerable private income. There is also some self-portraiture, Alice showing herself partly as she felt she was and partly as she felt she ought to have been. (According to her daughter she told Elgar that, for his sake, she wished she had been "really beautiful".)

In *The Portrait*, the hero, Charles Bernard, visiting a country-house (Hazeldine) in mid-summer meets Eveline Travers (Alice), a slight girl of three-and-twenty, orphaned niece of, and house-keeper to, the owner of the estate, in the garden. He falls in love on the instant and in due course marries her.

For Bernard it had been a long and hard road to matrimony. Alice noted how "he pondered over the many unhappy unions he saw in the Society in which he moved" before committing himself. It seemed to him that people "were too often carried away by a short lived passion excited by beauty or the more mercenary passion exploited by wealth". As he looked around Bernard reported of the girls put in his way, how "one was too frivolous, another too fond of outdoor sports, riding, hunting, etc., another paid too much attention to dress, another was dowdy, a fifth was illiterate, a sixth pendantic. . . ." The slight girl of three-and-twenty was none of these. How she appeared to others is within a conversation between two friends of Bernard, a Major Court and his sister Mary Rondell. In keeping with the spirit of the times both Court and his sister were victims of ill fortune, the one being a widower, the other a widow. Amazed that Bernard should seriously contemplate marriage, and being themselves not conspicuously intellectual, they were even more amazed at his intended bride. Court could only describe her as

> . . . a prodigy in every sense she is learned to a degree, a linguist, an artist, scientific besides, enthusiastic in attending all his committees and charitable meetings . . . and earnest without pedantry. . . .

Eveline like Alice (who makes sure that her readers know that she could read Schiller) was a Teutophile and the painter Herr Troter from Munich, responsible for the portrait which is the subject of the story and also of a good deal of misunderstanding in Court's mind, was doubtless a reflection of the fashionable Hubert von Herkomer, of whose paintings Alice was well aware.

Living in her dream world Alice saw herself as she would have wished to have been seen. There is one touching little passage concerning the Bernards at home in which she looks ahead, albeit unknowingly, to the actuality of her own life, and to

> the tasteful drawing room [where] the fire burnt brightly, the furniture offered a subdued glow of harmonious colours, the table was rich in a selection of books both old and new. . . .

An impression in water-colours of the drawing-room at Avonmore Road—the first home of the Elgars—is among the illustrations of this book.

Isabel Trevithoe: A poem, by C. A. R., was issued by the Charing Cross Publishing Company at the end of 1878 (although the imprint gave 1879 as the year of publication). A love story based in Cornwall (as a continuation of the response to Roden Noel and Porthcurnow), wrapped in idyllic, Tennysonian, blank verse, is not a masterpiece. This fact was cruelly noted by *The Sunday Times* on 26 January 1879. At the same time, as was more perceptively appreciated by the Scottish newspapers, the *Greenock Telegraph* and the *Falkirk Herald*, it had a significant political content.

Sir Stephen Trevithoe, whose estate was in Cornwall, died

> And left his only child alone, unwed,
> And homeless too, for strictly weighed th'entail
> On all his land . . .
> . . . Thus Isabel, from childhood used to wealth,
> A stranger to the thought that it might e'er
> Grow less, was now reduced to scanty means
> Compared to former years.

Once again Alice produces a young lady with geriatric responsibilities, and when she had been released from these she had others to face. However—at least in theory—she had a suitor. One day the virtuous Gilbert Ancillon would return from distant parts to claim his bride. Until that happy day, full of determination and resource, if lacking in relevant experience, she would go to London to help the poor and the sick. Conveniently she had an elderly widowed (!) cousin, Margaret, who would keep house for her in "hired rooms".

Behind Alice's narrative lies the imperative of Octavia Hill, from whose inspiring address of July 1876 she may well have drawn inspiration.

> . . . Have you ever realised what those acres of crowded, heated, badly-built houses, over which you pass so quickly by train when you go in and out of London, mean? What kind of homes they make, What sort of human beings live and die there? Have you asked yourselves whether your presence, your companionship, is needed there? Whether the little children want your teaching? Whether your gentleness, your refinement, your gaiety, your beauty, are wanted there? Neighbourhood! Oh yes, it has strong claims—some of the best possible; but then we must take care that we let our neighbours come round us naturally, rich *and* poor. I only know this neighbourhood as I see it from the station, and it is possible it is otherwise inside, for I know quarters where the poor lodge often escape the eye of a casual observer; but I do know districts which *are* very like what yours *looks*, where the villas cover all the ground, and there is no place for the poor man's cottage. Where the idea of building for him would be

mentioned with awed abhorrence by the comfortable residents, and they would talk about the unpleasantness of the poor living so near, chances of infection, etc. etc. Where the few persons required to serve the needs of the district live in a somewhat pampered and very respectful dependence in small districts withdrawn from view, visited and over-visited by ladies who haven't far to go—where the poor say there isn't a house to be had, and the rich say they get everything from a distance.[4]

In March 1878 the Secretary of State for the Colonies spoke in Cheltenham on Government legislation "on the subject of artisans' dwellings; to secure them better air, better houses, and homes that they might be proud to call their own". This speech was commented on in Arthur Arnold's article on "Socialism" in the same number of the *New Quarterly* that had carried Colvin's "The Apollo Belvedere".

Whatever her inspiration, Alice wrote how noble work

> Was found, and Isabel each day set forth
> To write and work in gloomy office-rooms,
> Beneath the rule of Lady President,
> Who gathered many such as Isabel
> To aid her in her task. . . .

In time the Lady President sent Isabel out "to wretched courts and dwellings, crowded close", to seek out those "long sunk in want and misery".

Cousin Margaret found all of this more than difficult to comprehend. In her day girls of her sort had only ever gone out duly chaperoned. But what, asked Isabel, happened to those whose parents did not need them, or those who had no parents? Margaret's immediate response was that she had never known such girls. It was well understood that young ladies of her generation, apart from occasional drives, or walks, or visits to selected households, were content to stay at home, to read—but not too much, to engage in needlework, to talk over the news—that is, who was dead, who was to be wed, how much Lady Elite's ball-dress cost, who was the new squire of. . . . Some of Jane Austen's England was still to be visited in Redmarley.

While Cousin Margaret commended contentment she opined that as a virtue it was out-of-date. She could not, however, dis-

[4] "A more excellent way of charity", *Macmillan's Magazine*, 1876, XXXIV, pp. 126–31.

guise a "slight contempt of change/Thus wrought by newer days".

Then Isabel,
Fresh fired to speech, would pour forth such a strain
Of burning words regarding women's work,
Their duties high, how they were bound to use
Their mighty influence to clear the world
Of wrong and endless sin, now half their fault,
And other thoughts all born of this new age. . . .

Margaret looked over her gold-rimmed spectacles at the girl "whose eyes with wakening fire flashed" as she spoke as she had to speak.

In the end Isabel was removed from the realities to which she had been consigned, and after various romantic improbabilities reunited with her lover, thereafter to live in happiness if not contentment.

Included within the narrative are two lyrics. One was an altered version of *The Snow* (see p. 63), the other, *Fly, singing bird*; both were to be given a longer lease of immortality in 1894 when set to music by Elgar.

From Pendock came a note of moderated appreciation from the Rector.

Friday 30 Nov [1878]

My dear Alice:
Mrs. Symonds and I have both been reading your pretty poetical story 'Isabel Trevithoe'. I am not a lover of blank verse and never was and read Milton more for duty than for love so I should have loved Isabel more if you had made her rhyme with the Lady Norah's sublime. I do not think that Gilbert quite deserves having two such nice girls in love with him. Again, you begged of me to criticise. I don't ever remember such an instance of *self sacrifice* as my Lady Norah's I mean in real life. If I did I would introduce it into my Essay on "The Influence of Woman on Man" and make the world richer by such an example of self denial.

Off with the old love!
On with the new!

is, as a rule, life outside of novels and poems.

Nevertheless dear Alice I quite agree with Mrs. Symonds when she says, "There are very few Girls, or Women, or Men who could write so pretty a tale as Isabel Trevithoe. I *am* sure *you* could not with all your philosophy". I must lend you Chambers' Journal with Harriet Davidson's[5] tale in it. There is a good deal of love in that but her romance of life soon faded poor child. What a lot of heart aches in this life that said love has caused!! That's an extract from "The Influence of Woman" etc.—the said influence will induce me to order some copies of Isabel & ask my friends to do so. Good bye dear Pupil.

Yours ever Affectly
W. S. Symonds

Symonds, alas! missed the main point of the poem.

In the April 1878 issue of the *New Quarterly* there was one other contribution of particular interest; a story by Thomas Hardy, "An Indiscretion in the Life of an Heiress". The durability of this work is destroyed by an appallingly sentimental deathbed ending. But in the delineation of Tollamore Church and School and of the countryside there is a good deal that reminds one of Alice, not least of her major work, *Marchcroft Manor*, published in July 1882—in which month the first reviews appeared.

Marchcroft is Alice's own country translated into the perpetuity of an endless summer. It was not far from Dorlcote Mill and if Alice is not of the rank of George Eliot, it is clear that she looked at some aspects of life with similar sympathies. A reviewer in the *Glasgow Herald*[6] responded kindly to the virtues of the book:

> We seem to have wandered into the fair pastoral land, with its rich woods and blue distances. We hear the fresh carol of the lark and the droning of the bees, we smell the new-cut hay, lie dreamily on the trim lawn, or watch the night flowers, from beneath the shade of the broad cedar. We even taste the thick cream of Mrs. Ruddock's farm, watch the cocks and hens with as eager delight as Dollie, or see the ducks sitting placidly near the water's edge....

But—remembering that only a year before *Marchcroft Manor* was published when Wilde's aestheticism was the vogue, *Patience* was performed for the first time—*The Academy*[7] suggests an artificiality of the kind that enchanted Gilbert: the book

[5] Harriet Miller Davidson (1839–83), daughter of Hugh Miller, writer and geologist, married Rev. John Davidson in 1869 and emigrated to Adelaide, Australia. The best of her writings was *A Man of Genius*.

[6] 14 September 1882.

[7] 29 July 1882.

is only to be described as an Idyll of the Affections. It is a somewhat measured and formal idyll, it is true, and an idyll of modern years: with an aesthetic barrister for one of its heroes, and an accomplished and engaging vicar to look on and play chorus. But its sentiment is idyllic, and its savour distinctly Arcadian.

The opinion of *The Academy* was endorsed by *The Athenaeum*. *The Standard*, *The Saturday Review*, as well as the *Glasgow Herald*, while not agreeing on the merit of the work stressed the liberal outlook of Selby, the vicar, and the radicalism of the hero, Julian De Tressanay. The political content of *Marchcroft Manor* is of particular interest in indicating how far removed Alice's thoughts were from those of the majority of those who were her daily companions.

The aesthetic barrister, Roger Osborne, one of the two heroes of *Marchcroft Manor*, is the friend of and foil to Julian De Tressanay, whose inheritance of the estate gives the title of the book.

An unusual point about De Tressanay (who held an appointment in the Foreign Office) is the stress placed by the author on his ethnic background. He was

> Unusually tall, his dark hair and olive complexion pointing to his foreign extraction. The expression of his face was singularly mobile, the dark eyes and rather irregular features lighting up with fire and excitement when speaking with eager gesture on subjects on which he felt strongly.

She also must have been aware of the significance of Benjamin Disraeli—who had died only in 1881—and De Tressanay would seem to have been an adherent to the tenets of Disraelian democracy. No doubt Alice had read *Daniel Deronda*, and had retained the image of its eponymous hero. This book had been published in 1876 and some of its other characters may be related to those of *Marchcroft Manor*; notably the rector of Denicote, the widowed Mrs. Harleth, and Gwendolen Harleth herself.

When Julian De Tressanay awoke to his good fortune he was somewhat shocked by it, expostulating:

> I, who have never thought of landed property, except to expatiate on the criminality of its tenure in general, and now I, of all people, I suddenly find myself the possessor of a large domain

Sir Henry Gee Roberts.
By an unknown artist.

Battle of the Banas River (Rajputana) between the British under Major-General Roberts and Tantia Topi

General Robert Napier Raikes.

Stanley Napier Raikes.

C. Roberts.

Hazeldine House, 1851.

Two pencil drawings by Julia Roberts.

View from the lawn at Hazeldine House, 3 July 1850.

The Rocks of the Dowards.

Pencil drawings by Sir William Guise,
Bart for *Records of the Rocks.*

Permian Braccia at Haffield, near Ledbury.

ırley
tot

Hardman
:hers in
llage
c. 1890.

and
:rs at the
: school,
o

Longhope.

Donnington.

Highnam.

Hasfield Court.

Birtsmorton Court.

Birtsmorton Church.

Mrs. Hyacinth Symonds.

Rev. William Samuel Symonds M.A

Pendock Church.

Lady Gertrude Thompson.

Mrs. Caroline Dighton.

Mrs. Vera Raikes.

Miss Roberts.

Redmarley D'Abitot Church.

The Rectory.

New Inn

Thorn Cottage.

Lady Roberts.

Alice, a camera portrait
by E. O. Hoppé, 1916.

Carice as a girl.

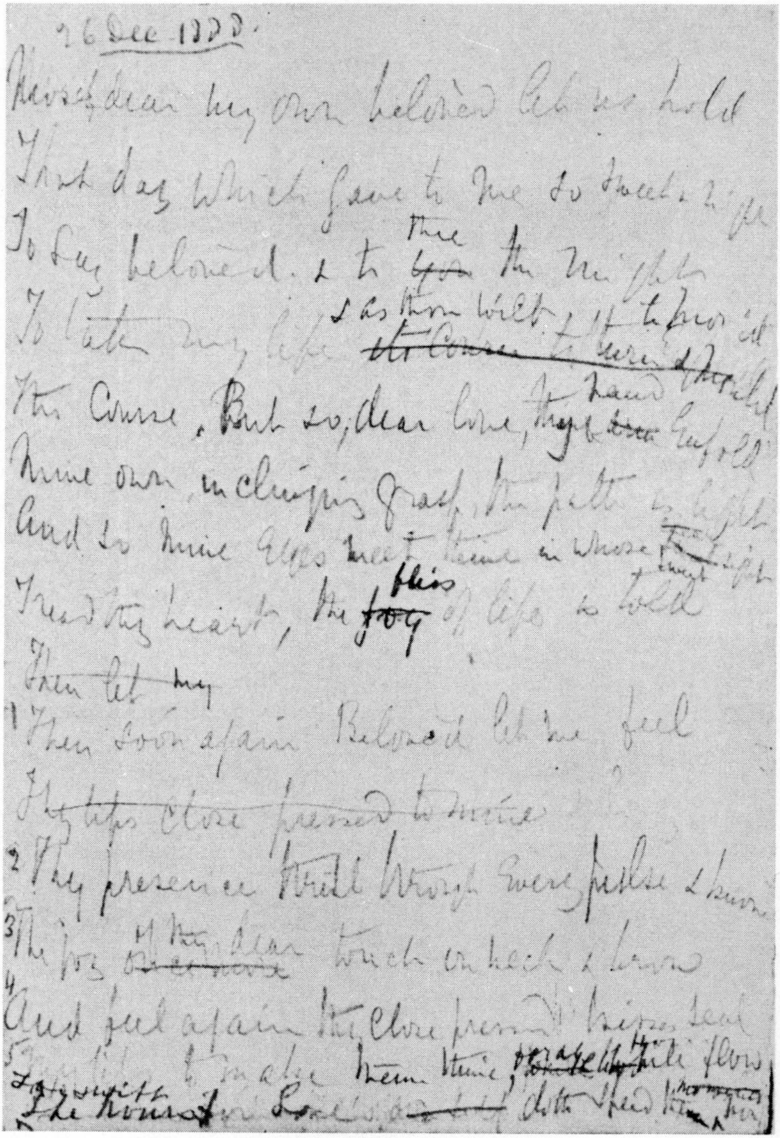
26 Dec 1888.

Most dear my own belovèd let us hold

Then soon again Belovèd let me feel

Most dear my own belovèd

I In Haven
(Capri)

Closely let me hold thy hand
Storms are sweeping sea & land
Love alone will stand

II

Closely cling for waves beat fast
Foam flakes ~~Scatter on the~~ cloud the hurrying blast
Love alone will last

III

Kiss my lips & softly say
Joy sea swift may ~~go~~ fade, ~~Sea swept~~, to day
Love alone will stay

Lady Roberts and Alice prepare to go visiting.

Lady Roberts and her children.

Edward, Carice and Alice, at Plas Gwyn, 1910.

and old Baronial mansion, every stone of which could probably bear testimony to the dread of violence and oppression committed by its rapacious feudal owners.

His friend, Roger, commented sardonically on such sentiments, but only succeeded in provoking Julian further:

It is a shame, Roger, it is really a shame that a man of your culture and enlightenment should speak with such persistent ridicule of the great movement of our age, the one attempt at progress which will distinguish this nineteenth century from other epochs.

Soon after De Tressanay had taken up residence at Marchcroft there was some discussion of politics in the Rectory. In response to his enquiry as to the opinions entertained by the villagers, Selby observed that in general their tendency was to let things be. This, thought Osborne, who was a party to the discussion also, was a good thing, but De Tressanay, while understanding that the newly enfranchised could hardly comprehend their political responsibility immediately, said:

. . . but we should do all in our power to enlightening them, and to impress them with the importance of the possession [of the vote], now for ever their own. . . . What should you say to a series of lectures, in a popular form, of course, on the franchise, and on the responsibility of each member of the commonwealth?

Selby considered that the harvest would occupy the minds of his parishoners to the exclusion of any such course in political education. In the winter, however, something might be done. But progress would be slow: "we must not," he warned, "expect to see immediate results or to see our efforts bear fruit in lives so short as ours".

Thinking one day on the possibility of sometime organising a party for the villagers in his park Julian wondered:

It will be so interesting to see if a carefully organised day of pleasure for the poor cannot be made a success in the country. Do you not think, Mr. Selby, that that class of people in England lead such dull, if not sad, lives, Even when tolerably well off they have no recreation. Their lives seem bounded by a tedious monotony which it is impossible for them to break through.

Selby, and more especially his niece Olive, contributed a gentle enthusiasm to De Tressanay's sociological musings. Olive was present one day when De Tressanay entertained his tenant farmers to luncheon, and heard him address them thus:

> I want you to look on me not as a man who has happened to become master of an estate, but as a friend who wants to learn your trials and troubles, that he may help you bear them, and thus the sum of them will be lightened feeling that we all belong to one great brotherhood, in which none has a right to be indifferent to the fortunes of another.

The model master soon learned that good intentions and progressive thoughts were as likely to gain the disfavour of many of those to whom they were directed. Farmer Diggle spoke for those who held do-gooders in deep suspicion. Longwindedly he expressed the thanks of the community for the luncheon and the speech, underlining that while none of them liked radicals and had "heerd" that the new squire was one of that class, the sincerity of his words had won their respect. Olive was afraid that Roger Osborne (whose girl-friend was Olive's sister, Ella) in his promised speech would undermine his friend's position by stating in public the cynical views he was apt to let loose in private. Roger, however, behaved himself commendably well, saying all the right things for the occasion.

At the end of the story De Tressanay married Olive and Ella married Osborne. The dénouement was never in doubt. But the real victory went to the radical spirit that at that time seems to have obsessed Alice Roberts. Nor did she mince her words:

> Julian never realized the prediction that Roger had made concerning him when he first succeeded to the Manor. He never lapsed into a common-place landowner with none but local interests. He became a distinguished politician and speaker. The old Conservative country gentlemen would shake their heads gravely and say, "A talented young man, it is a misfortune he should hold such dangerous views". Some of these grave personages, however, lived to find more than one of his audacious theories carried out and benefitting [*sic*] the community at large, although it was not to be expected that they should recognise the good these theories had effected after the dismal forebodings to which they had given utterance.
>
> In the course of time high honours and distinctions fell to De Tressanay's share . . . .

Like Hardy in his early story Alice was intent in *Marchcroft Manor* to display the range of her reading. Quotations from Tennyson, Matthew Arnold, Emerson, Dante, Hans Christian Andersen, Oliver Wendell Holmes, Homer, Spenser, Chaucer, and Shakespeare preface her chapters. At the head of Chapter VI, in which De Tressanay understands properly his feelings for Olive, Alice enigmatically put

* * * * * *

And wandered far and farther still,
They trod the vale and crossed the hill
And into fairy land.

On the manuscript of *Two Summers* Alice described herself as the author of *Isabel Trevithoe.* Like the poems that were published also in 1884 in *Home Chimes* the short story had been lying about for some time. The first of two summers was that of 1814, the subject the fate of the simple countryman in time of war. In this case it was the events surrounding the Battle of Waterloo that fired Alice's imagination. One day, during harvest time, George Rushton—betrothed to Mary Silverton—was picked up by a recruiting sergeant (à la Hugh the Drover, who also lived in Gloucestershire) in a public house in Haverton, the market town (Ledbury?) to which he had been sent on an errand by his master.

Before he could do anything about it (for he was treated to a "stupefying potion", which effectively anaesthetised him for a half a day and a whole night) George found himself not only far from home but also one of the King's soldiers. Alice knew well what kind of man George was, and what were his chances.

> There were no railways, no telegrams; there was a post indeed but schools had not been much thought of; and George Rushton could wrestle with any man in ———shire, climb the highest tree after a bird's nest, or hit a mark with his old father's gun; but as for reading and writing, he had no idea of either, and would have been fairly put to shame by a child of six from one of our modern day schools, taught of course by one of our certificated school mistresess. Thus, he was sent into the wide world, knowing as little where London was, with reference to his native village, as Dahomey; and his heart sickening at the thought of being sent over the seas—probably having a dim idea in his

mind that all foreigners were murderers and thieves, and would feast on him as well as kill him if they could get the opportunity.

Wounded at Waterloo, George was cared for by a Belgian peasant woman, whose deaf and dumb daughter, Marguerite, out of gratitude, he married. Marguerite produced a son, who, in turn married and fathered a son. At this point Marguerite died, thus leaving George, who had all but forgotten his native language, in limbo. Longing for the world he had lost, he was taken to Brussels, put on a train and given further directions which landed him in England. Somehow or other he reached Haverton and his native village, where all was the same, except that Mary—who had waited and waited for the return of her Ulysses—was, predictably, an old woman. In accordance with the sentimental requirements of the readers of *Home Chimes*, George fairly promptly "sank to his rest". No sooner was he interred than Mary's neighbour found her lying by the side of the new grave, "cold and still". She, like George, had passed to her rest.

The romantic story with a melancholy ending had a good innings. No doubt, a century after its genesis, *Two Summers* will catch the knowing sneer. But Alice, although hampered by its conventions, was able to inform it with her feelings for history, and for those whose labours supported the life-style of Roberts's, Raikes's, Probyns, *et al.*

5

The Consolation of Music

Marchcroft Manor was the high point of Alice's literary career. She was never again to try her hand at a novel. Insofar as she could have understood the term *Marchcroft Manor* was an essay in realism. Although couched in romantic terms, it dealt with life as it was when viewed from within the high tradition of Hazeldine; and precisely because of its limitations its value as a register of social conditions long out of sight is enhanced. It was also Alice's valediction to youth; for her there was no De Tressanay in prospect. She was, it seemed, inexorably destined to expiate the offence of being an only daughter by the seclusion of perpetual virginity. There were also at that time cold facts of death intruding into both private and public life.

In the spring of 1882 Fred Roberts, now a Major in the Royal (Bombay) Artillery, died, and was buried beside his father on the north side of Redmarley Church. Alice had been greatly devoted to this brother (whose presentation copy of *Isabel Trevithoe* is testimony of her affection), and his death at the early age of forty-one was a grievous blow to sister and mother. The proper prescription for grief was escape. Lady Roberts and her daughter therefore followed the practice of their kind. They left England and its—and their—woes behind, seeking therapy for their emotions in the sunny, romantic south. The bereaved ladies "revelled in seeing Rome and Florence (and Bordighera), and all the wonder and beauty they had spent such years in studying".[1] But the excursion was marred by both falling victim to "Roman fever" caused by inadequate sanitation.

Meanwhile changes were taking place at Redmarley. Henry Morton Niblett's induction as Rector took place on 24 May amid manifestations of satisfaction. He remained in that office until his resignation on 1 May 1925, and is well remembered

[1] from notes by Carice Elgar Blake.

as a kindly autocrat who faithfully visited his parishioners on foot, horse, or bicycle, through his incumbency. He taught his choirboys to swim in the River Leadon in the summer and by diligence at school to prepare themselves for the generally low state in which it would please God to call them. Niblett's young wife, Marian,[2] was quite a scholar too, and acted as governess to the Scobells of Redmarley.

In conjunction with Schoolmaster Toyne, who ruled the Upper School and lived at the Old Workhouse at the time, Niblett did his best to ensure that education was not too great a charge on the public. In 1887 the "families of the poorer classes" paid 2d. a week, "tradesmen and people in better circumstances" 4d. for the first child and 2d. for "any and each other of the same family", and "large farmers and people in still better position" 6d. The Parish Council levied a rate of 1d. in the £ for the maintenance of the village school. The problem of truancy and other forms of absenteeism was tackled according to a well-tried system. Every child who kept every attendance at school for a whole year was rewarded with a payment of 2s. Those who made more than 400 attendances also made 1s. 6d.

The same conditions did not apply in respect of church attendance. There are gloomy entries in the Register of Services. On 31 December 1882, for instance, Holy Communion at 8 a.m. was cancelled, there being "not sufficient members"; on 21 January following there was no Service "the church being full of smoke"; on 17 February 1884 the snow prevented the attendance of any of the parishioners. Insofar as numbers of communicants are a guide to intensity of belief it can only be said that those to whom Niblett ministered at the early morning service in the 1880's only rarely reached a total of twenty, and frequently there were only four present. Niblett was a stirring preacher who did not neglect to help his listeners to take account of their innumerable sins. In 1883 the Roberts's, still in Italy, missed a Lenten *tour de force* when the Rector delivered for the first time his set of seven addresses on the Seven Deadly Sins. John Lander, Rector of Donnington, Edward Chassall Scobell, Vicar of St. Luke's, Gloucester, and, of course, Symonds of Pendock,

[2] Marian, died in 1942, aged eighty-two.

were not infrequent visiting preachers, and the great occasion in the church's year was, naturally, the Harvest festival.

Shortly after Fred Roberts's death Alice wrote a piece, reminiscent of, but less evocative than, William Allingham, for a baby girl (of the Lander family?), "G.E.L. Born on All Hallow E'en".

What could the fairies bring thee then?
Were their gifts all forgot
Full sad were thy lot
On All Hallow E'en!
Nay, this dowry they brought
A strong spirit and true
To speak and to do;
Though the contest be keen
Of thy soul thou art Queen,
On All Hallow E'en.

On the whole the poem of which this is a part gives a poor recommendation to the infant for the world she had just begun to inhabit. In her next extant poem, written in Bordighera on 16 February 1883, taking Tennyson once again as exemplar in matters spiritual as well as poetical—Alice took a fashionably gloomy view of life.

Whither?

Flow the sails and flies the boat,
Skims the waves as shadow light,
Swift it speeds to port remote
Nor swerves nor slackens in its flight.

Gray the clouds as touched with care
Slowly heaves and sighs the sea,
Heaves and sighs whate'er may fare
Nor sad, nor glad, yet wearily.

O'er the wave of Time's swift tide
Swiftly speeds a human life,
Clouds and storms the track may hide
It may not pause though fierce the strife.

Goal unknown and haven past,
Refuge none upon the lee;
God grant it find a port at last
And rest from tossings of the sea.

Back from Italy and once more in residence at Hazeldine, Alice resolved to improve herself as musician. This, after all, was the supreme balm to hurt souls. With her mother she used to go by pony and chaise to Cheltenham, Gloucester, Malvern, or Worcester for concerts. Adolf von Holst and John Barnett and his talented family gave distinction to Cheltenham. In Gloucester Charles Lee Williams had just succeeded Charles Harford Lloyd as organist of the cathedral. There was in the city a Choral Society, of which T. Gambier Parry—Hubert Parry's father—was President, and W. Meath Baker—a friend of the Roberts's of some importance—an honorary member. There were as well a Madrigal Society and a Philharmonic Society. William Done was organist at Worcester. The two principal musical bodies here were the Philharmonic Society, which Done conducted, and the Musical Society, directed by A. R. Quaterman. Subscription concerts were organised by E. J. Spark, and the young Edward Elgar was in charge of the recently formed Worcester Amateur Instrumental Society. Elgar suffered the handicap of being the son of the principal of

> Elgar Brothers: Pianoforte and Music Dealers, Professional Pianoforte Tuners (by Appointment to Her late Majesty Queen Adelaide)
>
> 10 High Street.

As a secondary centre of musical culture—with domestic music-making of a high order, and *Unterhaltungsmusik* provided for tea-drinking dowagers by immigrant German musicians—there was Malvern. On 18 March 1886 Alice delivered herself of a poem suggesting her intellectuality and her status as a champion of the emancipated woman. (During this year the matter of Women's Suffrage was raised in Parliament in a Bill that did not pass a Second Reading). This was a time when Gilbertian concepts were in the air. The *Mikado* (1885) was much talked about. So we find Alice on her own model of a Starlight Express.

> What stay in the cold when a planet is there,
> 'Newgee' it is called though so far yet so fair:
> As seen through the glass 'tis a fair looking land
> With craters and geysers and hot looking sand.

'Tis warm for its denizens ramble about
In capes made of skins, or even without:
The place above all to get rid of our ills,
The snows and the frosts and the coughs and the chills.

Of Newgee their planet they'll make us a loan,
Poor things for they're still in the dull age of stone:
We'll take them torpedoes and matches of Mays'
We'll teach them the Code and Macaulay's proud Lays.

But now to be off by pneumatic airway
With snow and east wind we no longer will stay,
But shoot to Newgee in a month at the most
Though cold it will be midst the stars in their host.

Not one and two, but lo! thousand and three
Come eager to seek a lost sun in Newgee,
One clutches a vase and another a chair,
'A Sheraton', shrieks this aesthete with long hair.

'Their trains I'll soon teach them', cried one with a Brad-
Shaw, one oh so tenderly clasped his old Strad,
Declaring the Newgetes shall hear not a note
Save of futurist music both vague and remote.

Another brings tomes of statistical power,
Another declares he'll teach sad Schopenhauer,
Another expounds what a myth is the Dawn,
A fourth draws a plan of a good tennis lawn.

Then off they all went to enlighten Newgetes
With figures and patents and all the aesthetes:
And happy and warm are they there—for alas!—
No glimpse can we gain of our friends through the glass.

In this poem the most interesting reference is to the one who, clasping his violin, declared that the "Newgetes" would hear only "vague, remote, futurist music". In the West Midland environment, the music of the future was that of Wagner, Brahms, Dvořák, and Hubert Parry—the genius from Highnam Court, near Gloucester. But Parry was away in London, and agitation in and around Alice's territory was led by Edward Elgar, a young violinist and violin teacher who had been in Leipzig a few years previously, and had never ceased talking about the music and musical life of that city. Brahms was a principle enthusiasm and Elgar had written programme notes for some of Brahm's chamber works for the benefit of the people of Malvern.

> In 1886 [Alice] heard that there was a new and very brilliant teacher going over to Malvern weekly from Worcester to give lessons. After the lessons had been going on for some time the old coachman who had been with [the Roberts family] for many years, and who of course had to drive [her] into Malvern was heard to say that he thought "there was more in it than music".[1]

Alice is said to have become Elgar's pupil in pianoforte accompaniment on 6 October 1886. It is to be taken into account in this connection that however brilliant the young Elgar was as a teacher—and this is disputable, whereas his distaste for teaching is not—he was no keyboard specialist. That Alice had begun to think of him in romantic and proprietary terms is evidenced by a poem whose final version was made in the summer of 1887. The significance of this will become apparent in due course. The original title of *Despondency, a Remonstrance*, was altered to the more Augustan *An Admonition against Despondency*; the condition for which Alice prescribed in the following stanzas was one in which Elgar was frequently to be discovered.

Love the earth a little while,
For shadows swiftly flee across
Meadows lit with summer's smile,
Joy must not faint, all is not loss.

Love thy life, grief may not claim
To hold thy soul for evermore,
Nor with its touch thy spirit lame;
Demand the joy thou had'st before.

Art and music are thine own,
And thine the soul to whom must speak
The higher voices heard alone
By those who long and those who seek.

Gifts may come of friendship, love,
And human service gladness brings:
Rejoice, the sky is blue above
And hark! the lark exulting sings.

[1] Carice Elgar Blake MS.

Some time after her marriage Alice looked again at this poem and cabbalistically addressed her husband in a gloss: "I spec this is to E's own souse [?] Braut wopse", meaning "I expect this is to Edward's own self. Bride. . . ."

The pattern of Elgarian despondency in 1886 is contained in letters to Edward's Yorkshire friend, Dr. C. W. Buck, of Settle. Although he had enjoyed one or two gratifying moments of success at the end of 1885 it was apparent that any real fulfilment of creative ambition would be far in the future. Stockley, the Birmingham conductor who had been showing friendly interest in Elgar's music excused himself from undertaking a "Scottish Overture" which is no longer in existence. In January 1886 Elgar wrote his disenchantment to Buck:

> . . . I showed [the "Scottish Overture" to] old Stockley & he candidly said he could not read the score & it sounded to him disconnected. So I have retired into my shell & live in hopes of writing a polka some day—failing that a single chant is probably my fate.
>
> I am very lazy now have nothing to do & am *not doing* it. Begin again on the 25th. Fear our orchestral society is going —— to pot. People leaving etc.—I am a full fledged organist now &—hate it. I expect another three months will end it; the choir is awful & no good to be done with them.

In June, in a letter in which he invited himself to Yorkshire for a holiday, Elgar complained

> I have no work to do this term. I am cut out by my very good friends the Deutsches [German musicians, referred to on p.142, thought by many in Elgar's neighbourhood to be superior to any who were native].

But it was not all bad. There was Scap, the collie, which Elgar had brought back to Worcestershire from Yorkshire in 1885, and which was a source of innocent merriment for his "lady pupils". Among these Alice Roberts was assuming a place of some significance, and she went so far in declaring her interest in him publicly by inviting him to visit Hazeldine, where he underwent ordeal by afternoon tea under the scrutiny of Lady Roberts and other guests. In private Alice was far committed. On 25 March 1887, she emerged from her sitting-room with *Lyre and Song*, an intense reverie enshrining the artist's faith in his own destiny. This was the hard way to Parnassus.

Sound strong and clear my Lyre,
Flame in my heart my Song,
For joy can water no fire
The night of life is long.

I soared in fancy high,
I dreamed of love, renown;
Her bard elect was I,
And she, my chosen crown.

In raptured faith I took
A passionate long farewell,
While near us flowed the brook
And birds sang in the dell.

But love grew false and cold,
Fame proved an empty tale;
The dream of life is told,
The star of hope is pale.

Storm on though long the way
With sound of Lyre full strong;
Seek love and fame who may,
Leave me my Lyre and Song.

A few days later moral support was offered to the world in general, and Edward Elgar in particular, in a reflection on stoicism (indicative of reading of Matthew Arnold and George Long) entitled, *To emulate Marcus Aurelius*. The two opening stanzas offer the confidence to be obtained from eager devotion.

Too long and oh, too hard you say,
To reach such height,
And life is short for such assay
So small our might.

Stay not your heart with idle sigh,
So souled, you must
Seek something far, ere yet you die
And sink to dust.

On 13 May the Bishop of Worcester (although in the county of Gloucester the parish was under the ecclesiastical administration of Worcester diocese) came to Redmarley for a Confirmation Service. The church was filled as 106 candidates, of whom 57 were from Redmarley, were presented to the Lord Bishop. The Union Jack was raised on the tower for the occasion and the villagers were in joyful mood. They could also look forward to another festive occasion, for Whitsunday fell on 29 May. But the holiday spirit of the community became overcast. The bell was tolled on Whitmonday to mark the passing of Lady Roberts, who had lately become seriously ill. There was a brief Obituary in the *Ledbury Free Press* on 7 June, in which it was observed:

> . . . her loss will be deeply felt in the neighbourhood, where her kindness to the poor had made her deservedly beloved. She leaves one son, Stanley Napier, Major in the King's (Liverpool) Regiment, and one daughter.

In that may be heard the characteristic sound of Victorian charity, of the rustle of the black silk dress. In her last years Lady Roberts was looked after by the faithful Sarah Allen, who stayed in Alice's service, and then that of the Elgar household until her death in 1923. In 1887 there was another break with the past. W. S. Symonds died in Cheltenham and on 18 September he was buried in Pendock, where the funeral service was conducted by Robert Pilson, Rector of Birtsmorton. Stained glass was subsequently put in the west window of Pendock Church in memory of Symonds. There were already windows commemorating his father, his mother, his sister (who died in 1874) and his father-in-law.

Freed at last from her daughterly tasks, Alice fled from Redmarley, from the great empty house, and took up residence in "Saetemo", a rented property in Malvern.

6

The Course of True Love

At the end of 1887 Edward Elgar's prospects appeared little brighter. Of the small talk of provincial music he was tired; by its irrelevancies quite disenchanted. The "average taste in Music", he wrote to Frank Webb with reference to the Worcester Amateur Instrumental Society of which he was conductor, "is extremely low". He had instituted a Ladies' Orchestral Class, "with sixteen fair fiddlers all in two rows". The performance of his *Three Pieces for Small Orchestra* which had been promised by Stockley was postponed. He had written a great deal of music, but none of it looked commercially significant.

It was not all gloom, but for Alice, still wearing mourning, the darker side of the artistic temperament held a special appeal, The role of tragic heroine was an appealing one to a lady who not only had had recent cause for sorrow but who had a personal conflict to resolve; that existing between physical urgency and moral imperative. There was another source of conflict to appear soon, between the claims of Canterbury—as deposited at Redmarley D'Abitot—and Rome. At this time Elgar was still organist of the Roman Catholic Church of St. George, Worcester, and still unenthusiastic.

A month after the death of Symonds Alice wrote *Renunciation*—a draft for a farewell to love. It ended in this manner:

> My sweet, love is lingering round thee,
> Though blindly thou passest by,
> Not dreaming of sorrow so near thee,
> My dole, from thy hand, for aye.
>
> But now, lest a word should surprise thee,
> I'll bury love out of sight,
> Deep down lest a sigh it might cost thee
> Deep down, in the dark of night.

But in another poem, a sonnet entitled *Ways to the Mount*, composed on 9 October, Alice expressed herself more optimistically. There were, she suggested, many ways to the ultimate of perfection, but it is for each of us to choose a right way. Having done so and travelling along it

> We find the goal where love will all atone.

On 19 November *A Benison* was written, and uniquely authenticated by the signature Al[ice]. This sad little piece reflects on a theme to be developed later in a wider context: the perils of success and within it an implicit threat of alienation. At this time, however, Edward, for whom survival was the main aim, was not likely to have been receptive to such advice.

Dear and beloved, may all be well with thee,
And all the way thou walkest glimmer bright
With happy radiance thy glad eyes may see,
And God's own sunshine touch thy life with light.

(But my deep benison thou ne'er wilt know,
My heart may break, not thine, to say farewell,
Dear[1] friends are with thee, kindly[2] greetings flow,
Though[3] none perchance, but I, love thee so well.)

May pleasant[4] gifts of earth be thine, not coarse
Or heavy joys to clog thy soul with ease,
Or[5] yet success, or fame, if bought with loss
Of sinking to a lower art to please.

And twixt thee and the chilling world, be thine
A home, where love shall light the darkest day,
Where tender thoughts thy every step entwine
And tender words shall gladden all thy way.

My prayer would farther reach, O dear my friend—
Be thine to find some Paradise of light,
When time must gently shadow forth the End
And bear thee for a while, beyond our sight.

[1] *Glad Dear*
[2] *happy*
[3] *But*
[4] *goodly*
[5] *Nor* deleted from first draft.

On 30 January 1888, Alice was far from giving up any claims she may have supposed herself to have on Edward's affections. In another sonnet she wrote a free fantasia on the theme "The Friend of the Bridegroom . . . rejoiceth greatly", from St. John's Gospel (3, 29), seeing how the bride

> . . . stands his own, for always at his side.
> The closest of his friends must too be near,
> A friend so true, who loves with love so dear
> His heart can in the bridegroom's bliss abide.

The "closest friend", maybe, was Hubert Leicester, the Worcester printer with whom Elgar had been intimately acquainted from boyhood. The next composition the charming, neo-Jacobean, *O Happy Eyes* took on an added significance when, after slight modification both by poet and musician, it was turned into a part-song[6] On 4 March Alice (and Edward?) attended Divine Service in Worcester Cathedral. Canon Knox Little (1839–1918), an Irishman from Co. Tyrone, who had just given up a Residentiary's stall for the Vicarage of Hoar Cross, in Staffordshire—where Bodley's new church was the proper receptacle for Knox Little'e eloquence—was the preacher.

His sermons were listened to by discriminating congregations both in Britain and in the United States. Some of those delivered in St. Paul's Cathedral, in London, and in Trinity Church, on Wall Street, in New York, were published in *Sunlight and Shadow*, in 1889. Knox Little was capable of resonant commination. Calling people to repentance, and reminding his immediate audience of the consequence of exploitation, he delivered a sermon on the theme of Judgment one day that still has validity.

> Men who had eyes to see should not fail to notice that the misgovernment of ages, the forgetfulness of what was due from man to man, the oppression of the weak, the selfishness of the powerful, the heartlessness of the proud, were leading to a social upheaving of unusual awfulness, and at last the crash came.

[6] *O Happy Eyes* was accepted for publication by Novello & Co. Ltd., on 23 February 1894. On 22 March 1894 they took an "assignment of Miss [*sic*] Elgar's words", and paid the composer three guineas for the song which appeared as a *Musical Times* supplement in March 1896.

That referred to the decline and fall of tyrannies in the past, but so it would be in the not distant future unless the lessons of the past were properly learned.

On 4 March 1888 Knox Little thundered another warning down through the nave of Worcester Cathedral. "It is," he started, "appointed to all men to die once". Moved by the preacher, and agreeing from her own experience with another of his sentiments, that "in the Christian life, as in the Christian revelation, there are dark shadows as well as the light of morning", she went home and paraphrased his message into another sonnet. Eight weeks later melancholy, and the thought of rejection and consequent repinement, brought a bleak poem into being, of which the saddest sounds are in these stanzas:

I wonder if ever the crowds as they sway
And surge like the tide, if they ever will bring
That face that I know. They carelessly fling
    Down street and down square
    And leave me to fare
With the wound in my heart alway.

The sounds they are troubling and far is the way
(I listen to voices and speech)
    And I long for one song
    As I journey along
With the wound in my heart alway.

One song and one voice though they never may reach
My listening ear in the tumult that sways
And burdens the weeks and the nights and the days
    I hearken in vain
    And I journey again
With the wound in my heart alway.

The voices that Alice heard were those of a miscellany of relatives, raised in unmelodious defamation of her musician friend.

In the meantime Edward's Suite had been played in Birmingham and—although the gilt was removed somewhat from the gingerbread by its attribution of the work to "Mr. Algar"—commended by *The Musical Times*. On 7 May Edward Vine Hall (b. 1837), a Minor Canon of Worcester since 1877, a former chorister of New College and Magdalen College, Oxford, and a keen amateur musician, conducted Elgar's new *Suite for String*

Orchestra—comprising "Spring Song", "Elegy", and "Finale"—at a Worcestershire Musical Union concert. The score did not survive, but its memory does, in Alice's lines:

The strains arise
And swell to subtle melodies:
They tell of far and flowery meads,
Of rivers fringed with wavering reeds,
Of hills awaking to the Spring.
Of all the pleasant sights fair earth may bring.

But lo! they seem
Hushed to a finer, mystic dream.
The weaving rhythm of the song
Ascends and bears the soul along;
To loftier rapture must it soar
Which sounds of earth can satisfy no more.

And love and pain
Now mingle in the strain again,
While mystically the music swells,
Floats on and on, and ever tells
Of joy and love, and yearnings past:
Of hopes divine and longings vast;
No instrument could breathe it all
So subtle, strange, the harmonies that fall.

At least Alice may be heard to echo general principles within the Elgarian aesthetic. The meads, rivers, and hills were "far" only by poetic licence; in reality they were those of Worcestershire. The second stanza even preludes a greater "mystic dream", as of *Gerontius*, Newman's

. . . grand, mysterious harmony:
. . . like the deep and solemn sound
Of many waters

is of the Elgarian kind presaged by Alice, whose idealisation of "subtle, strange" harmonies was turned into a lasting reality before the passing of much more time.

In July the first joint work of Alice and Edward was published; his setting of *The Wind at Dawn*, a prize-winning entry for a competition organised by Joseph Williams for *The Magazine of Music*. At the end of August Edward went to Settle to stay with the Bucks.[7] Before he went Alice wrote a memorial to her feelings, chaste and lightly tinted with the sensibility of her favourite Pre-Raphaelites. *Love's Grace* was dated 16 August.

It chanced one day
My feet led me a happy way,
A way most sweet, for so it fell
That I upon my Love did light
Which made that joyful road most bright.
The gladness in me wrought, no words can tell.

O blessed day
Whose hours drew me along that way,
For soothely then my Love did smile
And by Love's favour did I stand
One instant's time, yes, hand in hand.
My heart will feast to think of that long while.

'Tis gone the day
Which set me on such favoured way,
Enough forme, most thankful slave
Such joy in that glad hour I seized
For truth to tell my Love looked kind
With thankful heart I keep Love's grace in mind.

After his return from Settle—whereabout at this time he composed his complement to *Love's Grace* in *Liebesgrüss*—Edward wasted little time in proposing formally to Alice, to whom his new piece was dedicated. On 22 September he wrote in his diary, "Engaged to dearest A."

This news brought cries of horror from the Roberts & Raikes (with the notable exception of Mr. & Mrs. W. A. Raikes and her mother who lived in Norwood and were always most helpful). They said he was an unknown musician; his family was in trade; and anyway he looked too delicate to live any length of time. One of the aunts was going to leave Alice a substantial sum, but

[7] Charles William Buck met Elgar at a B.M.A. Conference in Worcester in 1882. The two men enjoyed a friendship for fifty years—as the extant correspondence shows. Buck practised medicine in Settle, in Yorkshire. He played in an amateur orchestra at Barnoldswick, was President of the Bolton Musical Artists (Society)—to whom he once read a paper on Dvořák—and of the Settle Naturalists' and Antiquarian Society founded by Thomas Brayshaw (see below p. 99), and Churchwarden of Settle Parish Church, at various times.

on hearing the news, she forthwith cast her out of her will altogether.[8]

The rest of the year passed by according to established pattern. At the Three Choirs Festival, at Hereford, the principal works performed were *Messiah, Elijah, The Golden Legend,* and *Blest Pair of Sirens.* Both Sullivan and Parry, who later were to show much kindness to Elgar, were present to conduct their own works. At the beginning of October Elgar composed a motet, *Ecce Sacerdos magnus,* in honour of the visit of Bishop Ilsley, of Birmingham, to St. George's Church, Worcester. Two days later, on 11 October, Elgar went to Hanley to play in the orchestra for the first of the North Staffordshire Festivals. He was a member of practically every orchestra assembled in the West Midlands at that time, a fact which, as much as any other, explains his later supreme mastery of orchestral colouring. But it was a hard-won mastery. Professional demands were inexorable, but social security for a provincial professor of music depended largely on the suffrages of women whose continuity of ennui was relieved by classical music, and whose sexual urges often led them to appropriation of the affections of its practitioners. Elgar not only had his Ladies' Orchestral Class, but also a choral society for female singers in Malvern. His other duties included orchestral conducting in Worcester and directing the music at St. George's. If there was time to spare he was welcome in one or two of the houses in Malvern where chamber music was both practised and appreciated. But in the winter months there was little opportunity for a private life.

There is, however, a memory of the climax of the year in some pencilled lines of Alice, written on Boxing Day. . .

Most dear my own belovèd let us hold
That day which gave to me so sweet a right
To say belovèd & to [you] thee the might
To take my life [its course to turn and mould]
& as thou wilt to mould
Its course. But so, dear love, [thine arm]
thy hand enfold
Mine own, in clinging grasp, the path is light
And so mine eyes meet thine in whose [clear] sweet sight

[8] From Carice Elgar Blake MS. notes.

I read thy heart, the [joy] bliss of life is told
[Then let my]
Then soon again Belovèd let me feel
[Thy lips close pressed to mine]
Thy presence thrill through every pulse & know
The joy [once more] of thy dear touch on neck & brow
And feel again the close pressed kisses seal
My lips to make them thine for aye. While flow
Too swift the hours for Love doth speed them now.

The last two lines demanded much use of the rubber. But it was not every woman who could even then greet her love in a sonnet cast in the manner of Petrarch.

7
Mixed Marriage

There was a good deal of activity at the beginning of 1889. Alice and Edward were both in London, where—in view of the pressures imposed by provincial snobbery and in answer to surgent ambition—they determined to settle after marriage. On 26 January Edward took a further step towards the realisation of this intention by giving to his fiancée an engagement ring, with six little pearls. For the remaining months of winter, and through the spring, the routine was as before, Edward playing at St. George's on Sunday, rehearsing the Ladies' Orchestral Class on Wednesday, and the church choir the same evening, with obligations to play in the Festival Choral Society Orchestra on Monday and the Birmingham orchestra on Thursday. Quite often, however, there were visits to the Fittons at "Fairlea"—a musical stronghold in Malvern.

Mrs. Harriet Margaret Fitton was a daughter of Dr. George Gregory, himself an amateur musician from a Scottish family distinguished academically and scientifically, and notably interested in music. She had studied music in Germany, and also with Henry Brinley Richards, who had once taken lessons with Chopin. She was accompanist to the Worcestershire Musical Union—which Vine Hall conducted—and to the Herefordshire Philharmonic Society. Those who assembled at Mrs. Fitton's musical afternoons or evenings included her daughters (one of whom, a cellist, was the wife of Rev. Edward Capel-Cure, Elgar's librettist for *Lux Christi*), Vine Hall, and a Birmingham Oratory priest Henry Bellasis (a friend of Cardinal Newman, and in due course of assistance to Elgar in preparing a libretto from *Gerontius*), E. W. Whinfield, a local organ builder, Arthur Quaterman, John Austin, as well as Alice and Edward. Alice had known Mrs. Fitton (who had come to Malvern in 1868) for a long time and they were good friends, "their unusually cultured minds being in close sympathy with each other".[1] Mrs. Fitton was in a minority of friends who, if not actually excited at the prospect of Alice's marriage to Edward, were not positively unsympathetic.

For Alice marriage meant the end of one road. In view of the fact that not all women achieved this once principal aim of womanhood, she was in one sense a success. It was, however, a success achieved at the very last minute. Forty years of age she could not hope to capture a man's affections by glamour—her lack of which caused her, according to her daughter, to lament for Edward's sake. She was in *alter ego* Isabel Trevithoe, possessed of a stock of knowledge that was a commendation to some if an impediment to understanding by others. But Alice's secret writings (poems by their nature are private) show emotional and intellectual qualities in combination with a passionateness that the later image of "Lady Elgar" totally disguises.

It is surprising, perhaps, in view of the closeness of their association that mention of Alice only occurs in Edward's letters to Charles Buck at a late date. It is clear, however, that she had been talked about.

Worcester. Feb. 15: 1889.

My dear Charlie,

Very many thanks for photo: & instructions wh: I have sent on to [William] Grafton. Give my kind regards to Brayshaw & hope he is better.

Now!

Far from being mouldy I am gay: *we* are to be married about end of April & settle in London! All things fixed except date.

I am in great haste so will leave you to think over that much please give all good messages to Mrs. Buck & Morton & presently "calling the rest of the house together thank the Lord you will be rid of a knave"!

Otherwise the knight of the rueful countenance no longer.

Yrs. afftc.
E. W. Elgar!!
God wot!

[1] E.A.G. in Obituary of Mrs. Fitton in *The Malvern News*, 26 January 1924.

Edward and Alice had many things going against them. Although she was the elder, he himself—according to life expectancy and the time chart of the period—was not all that young. Nor, as yet, was he at all successful—a serious offence against the middle-class canon. He was hypochondriac and subject to disturbing mood changes. He wanted to conquer the Worcestershire bourgeoisie and to be accepted by them; at the same time at heart he despised them and their values. In that he was an artist there is nothing very strange about this, but it meant that there were many problems in store for a woman intending to engage herself in his career. But, it should be added, Alice too was an artist, and by no means the kind of woman she ought to have been if she had obeyed the conventions of which she was a victim. There was another major problem in this marriage—the difference of religion. Within the context of nineteenth-century Evangelical churchmanship such as was preached to Alice by the Nibletts, Scobells and Landers across the years, there was little opportunity for a mixed marriage to be other than a disaster—even if the non-Catholic partner were to succumb to the blandishments of the Scarlet Woman.

Alice prepared herself for marriage under such unpromising conditions by tacit surrender of her own past to the ghosts of Hazeldine. She would forget the dreams of fulfilment through social reform and alliance with high-minded radical idealism, incorporated in *Isabel Trevithoe, Marchcroft Manor*, and *The Portrait*, and live out another dream. She would make it her duty to create the conditions for genius to emerge. She would become both wife and surrogate for Edward's mother Ann, who so far had inspired and driven him on.

The marriage took place at Brompton Oratory at noon on 8 May. As Alice was not a Catholic the ceremony was a brief one. Edward's parents were present. Charles Buck came down from Yorkshire for the occasion. Most of Alice's relatives were ostentatiously absent, representation of her side lying exclusively with Willie and Veronica Raikes. Raikes was a barrister and was always to hand, so far as the Elgars were concerned, with sound professional advice. Another friend of Alice, a Mrs. Marshall, helped to make the occasion properly memorable by arranging a wedding breakfast at her house, at 72 Drayton

Gardens. The happy pair then went for a three week honeymoon to the Isle of Wight, some part of which was spent in Ventnor. The death of Elgar in 1934 released many anecdotes and recollections, among which, in the form of a letter to his daughter, was a letter from Miss Horsford, the daughter of the Ventnor landlady who had entertained the newly wed Elgars.

> Sir Edward and your mother had the drawing-room floor & won all our praise for their simplicity and lack of ostentation or "swank". I remember they left a very appreciative & flattering account of their visit to us which I would give a good deal to have preserved. . . . The recollection of your great father's visit will be green in my memory until my own call comes.

The landlady's daughter started at the end rather than at the beginning; the Elgars in 1889 had very little about which to "swank". From the Isle of Wight they returned to London and until the end of July lived in rooms.

At Redmarley in the meantime there was another wedding that created much interest, and since it took place in regular manner in St. Bartholomew's Church it created both work and pleasure. Dr. Frank Hayes Smelt, of Newent—son of Thomas Smelt, Gentleman (as the Register had it)—a forty-year-old general practitioner, married Maud Mary Symes, a widow, daughter of William Simkin (Gentleman), of Redmarley. The bride was well connected, being a Stokes on her mother's side, and was given away by her uncle, Henry Stokes. Her brother, Robert Simkin, curate at Dymock, assisted the Rector of Redmarley to perform the ceremony.[2]

On 10 June Alice wrote to her "Dear friends at Redmarley" thanking them for the water-colour painting of Redmarley which had been their wedding present. She also intimated her wish to give two prizes for the best flower borders, to be competed for by Redmarley residents at Eastnor Flower Show. Edward also played part in writing thank-you letters.

3 Marloes Road W
June 11 : 1889

My dear Charlie & Mrs. Charlie,

You will wonder what had come to me! I called at Rathbone

[2] There is a picture of Dr. Smelt on his rounds in Gordon Winter, A *Country Camera*, 1844–1914, London 1966.

pl:[3] on Friday & found your splendid present: & got them to send it down & now the three pieces grace our drawing room & are the most admired things in it.

Please accept our most hearty thanks for the prettiest things we have, we are never tired of looking at them.

I sent a little note, I think, from Ventnor,[4] but of course I was not alive to the fact the china existed then.

Love to you all: hope you are well & have enjoyed the splendid weather now past!

Adieu: let me hear sometime & be sure [to] come here if in town & reiterate our message to the family.

Yours ever
Ed. W. Elgar

There followed a holiday in Malvern, where there was recreational chamber music both at the Fittons and at Edward Nevinson's—whose cousin Basil played the cello. Alice was commended for her piano playing. There was no intention of staying in Malvern beyond the point at which they could move into the Raikes's house in Norwood. This had been offered as a London base while the Raikes's were in India in the hope that during that time the Elgars might find a place of their own. Oaklands, in College Road, Upper Norwood, was pleasantly situated, with a woodland view. It was not far from the Crystal Palace, where, in addition to concerts, there were frequent art exhibitions as well as Dog and Cat Shows. Elgar used to say afterwards that whatever he had learned about Greek and Italian architecture he had learned at that time at the Crystal Palace. The Dulwich Art Gallery was another source of interest in the vicinity. But so that Edward could pursue his proper concerns a grand piano was sent up from Worcester.

On 6 October the Elgars were again in Malvern, and while Alice was at church Edward wrote to Buck. His letter contains an enigmatic observation which invites a variety of psychological glosses, but no certain conclusions:

> . . . And now (after all our talks about the mystery of living) I must tell you how happy I am in my new life & what a dear, loving companion I have & how sweet everything seems & how

[3] John Beare (1847–1928) son of a Settle lawyer, musical instrument dealer of Rathbone Place, London, a business connection of Elgar Bros, was Buck's brother-in-law.

[4] See *Letters of Edward Elgar*, ed. Percy Young, 1956, p. 43.

understandable existence seems to have grown: but you may forget the long discussions we used to have in your carriage when driving about but I think all the difficult problems are now solved and—well I don't worry myself about 'em now!

In November Edward's *Liebesgrüss*, conducted by August Manns, was played at a Crystal Palace concert. Edward was not there. Instead he was in the Midlands, playing in a concert in Birmingham, and rehearsing in Worcester and Hereford. Alice, however, accompanied by Edith Lander, was able to be at the Crystal Palace. Within limits life was proceeding in a more or less promising manner, although the Elgars needed to work on a fairly tight budget. Edward had managed to pass one or two minor pieces to publishers, and when he felt depressed Alice was there to alleviate the situation. There was, for instance, a difficulty with Andrew Lang over Elgar's wish to publish his setting of *My love dwelt in a Northern Land.* At first, Lang refused permission to allow his words thus to be used. But Alice was fully equal to this emergency.

Afar, amidst the sunny Isles
We dwelt awhile, my love and I;
The sea stretched blue for endless miles
And seldom ships went floating by,
So hushed and still were wave and sky.

When moonbeams 'cross the billows lay
We watched together on the shore;
We longed the hand of time to stay
And linger here for evermore,
Such hours had been but dreamed before.

The breezes wafted scents afar,
Bright garlands flung their blossoms high;
Nought seemed the deep-breathed peace to mar
Till night came like a whispered sigh,
The light of day might scarcely die.

The Isles still cluster in the west
I nought of their fair skies can tell;
The sun may flush the mountain crest
But death below its shade must dwell;
There nought can touch my Love at rest
Beneath the blue waves' surge and swell.

Edward wrote a note above the final draft of this poem:

When A. Lang refused permission (afterwards granted with a very bad grace) to use "My Love dwelt in a Northern Land" "Madame Alice" wrote this to fit the music.

E. E.

Very clever

On 13 December Alice wrote her valediction to an eventful year and greeted that which was approaching in another sonnet: *For New Year, To E. E.*

The night is still, the Year moves to its end;
The happy Year which, slowly day by day
Drew thy dear soul and mine the selfsame way. . .

A week later Edward wrote to Buck:

Oaklands,
Fountain Road,
Upper Norwood S.E.
Dec. 21; 1889

My dear Charlie,

Our little greetings with this: I add the little card for your especial behoof. Very many thanks for the lovely photo; of the old Scars, it is installed in a place of honour & much admired: Alice is longing to see the original & some day we are hoping to drop down on Settle en route somewhere Scotswise: but that can't be yet. I found the photo at Rathbone Place on Tuesday & promptly confiscated it: what a whale you are not to have let me know you were coming up! & did you ever get a little score I sent you.

Will you give my kind regards to Mr. Brayshawe (J. of that ilk) & good wishes for the season also hang over other spiritual vessels who may be appearing.

John was coming to dine with us on Friday & flute generally but is, I am very sorry to find, laid up with an eye trial. I hope to call and see him tomorrow.

Give my kind regards to Mrs. B. & kiss the family with much love to yourself & kind regards to you all from my wife

Believe me,
Ever affecly yrs
Edward Elgar

There was a flaming account of me in the Telegraph last Friday & you didn't see it ! !

The "flaming account" here referred to appeared in *The Daily Telegraph* on Friday, 13 December 1889, and ran as follows:

Some curiosity having been expressed as to Mr. Edward Elgar, to whom the committee of the Worcester Festival have applied for a new orchestral work, the following facts may prove interesting: Mr. Elgar is no novice in orchestral composition. He has written several things of importance, among them a suite in four movements, and a set of pieces for strings only, which have been produced at Mr. Stockley's Concerts in Birmingham.

Other works have been performed at the Crystal Palace Daily Concerts, under the direction of Mr. Manns, and still others are to be found in the catalogue of Messrs. Schott and Co. The fact that besides proved ability, Mr. Elgar is a native of Worcester, and was till last May a Professor in the Town, may be taken as sufficiently explaining the action of the Festival Committee.

Soon after New Year Alice knew that she was pregnant, and also that they had no home of their own. In depressing weather Edward walked about the suburbs of London until he was foot-weary. Each day seemed more hopeless than the last. Surprisingly his spirit stood up and his discontents were diverted into a humorous statement of his views on Estate Agents, done up trochaically and tetrametrically in this manner:

I shd. tell you,—
"In the breezy heights of Hampstead,
In the Classic Highgate's Archway,
In the mediaeval Bromley,
In the precincts round by Barnum,
All the Agents sang unto me
Of the houses & the gardens
In most melancholy suburbs,
And the noisiest of streets."
If still further you should ask me
Saying, "What House Agents are they
Tell me of these siren singers,"—
I shd. answer your inquiry
Straightway in such words as follow:
"In the ague-tainted Chiswick
(Once a green & silent valley),
By the smelling water-courses
Have I lived & toiled & suffered.
And the foul-smelled water-courses
I have traced them through the valley
To the Johnson-haunted Streatham
With its jerry-builded houses
And its style of quasi-Queen-Anne,
Full of hope & full of heartbreak,—

And the foul-smelled water-courses
I have traced them through the valley
To the Johnson-haunted Streatham
With its jerry-builded houses
And its style of quasi-Queen-Anne,
Full of hope & full of heartbreak;—
But I never found the Agents'
Siren-songs are not-fulfilled;
Mere delusions, sad & sorry,
Found I ever, everywhere—
But I sometimes in my Rambles
Through the foul lanes they had sent me
Paused by some neglected graveyard
For a while to muse & ponder,
And I thought & whispered softly:—
"What a lying lot they are!"

E. E. 19 Jan: 1890

Oaklands

After a week's house hunting—

But I never found the Agents'
Siren-songs one jot fulfillèd;
Mere delusions, sad & sorry,
Found I ever everywhere—
But I sometimes in my Rambles
Through the foul lanes they had sent me,
Paused by some neglected grave-yard
For awhile to muse & ponder;
And I thought & whispered softly,—
What a lying lot they are!"

E. E. 19 Jany.
1890
Oaklands

After a week's house hunting

On 24 February the obliging Manns played the *Sevillana Suite* at a mid-day concert at the Crystal Palace, and a month later Elgar took a three year lease of 51 Avonmore Road, West Kensington, the agreement being signed in Sergeants' Inn in the office of a solicitor named Lander, of the Gloucester family of that name. On 20 April wrote her gratitude to her cousin's wife in two gentle stanzas:

Fair breaks the Spring o'er copse and mead
And sunshine steeps the gladsome land in light;
She willingly our wondering steps would lead
To fairer scenes, unknown to wintry night.

So let these strains attune your soul, and bring
Soft floating sounds from restful spheres, afar
From din of circling hours: they fain would sing
Of peace, and those high joys no strife may mar.

These were copied into the copy of the Organ Voluntaries (Op. 14), which were published that year by Orsborn and Tuckwood, given to Vera Raikes, who twice recalled the occasion in letters of 1923(?) to Carice Elgar Blake:

. . . I have several of [Alice's] poems & a sweet thing of hers, wh. *he* set to music "for 'Vera' " but only quite a little thing of course! . . .

(Feb 2)

. . . I enclose the little manuscript of music & y. dear mother's little sweet poem (sent me after that winter they spent at *Oaklands*. . . .

Alice and Edward prepared for their new home by ordering gas fittings from the Army and Navy Stores, carpets from Liberty's, beds from Maple's, and blinds from Hampton's, and arranging with the Army and Navy Auxiliary Stores about the removal. Some furniture, as well as books, came from Malvern, especially some of the Indian furniture that had once graced Hazeldine and the house Alice had rented in Malvern. The move took place on 24 March, the day being made more difficult in that one of the two maids then employed by the indigent Elgars fell ill.

The change of address was notified to the Bucks.

51 Avonmore Road
West Kensington W
Ap: 6 1890

My dear Charlie,

We have at length settled down to a permanent abode & the above will be our address for the future: we have taken this little house for three years & have, during the last three weeks, been settling our furniture & making things comfortable as far as possible, but it is a long & weary work & there remains much to be done, but we are ready to see you whenever you come to town & Mrs. B. & the family: let me know when there is a chance of seeing you. I have fixed up the phots: of the 'Scars' & all the other little bits of Settle country which I remember so dearly well: by the way, at the Photographic Exhibit^{n}. at the C. palace a few weeks ago some enterprising soul sent 8 or 9 photos: of Settle & district including 3 of the Market place, showing the N[aked] M[an] Hotel but not yr. house: I went and gazed at 'em many times: Gordale, Weatherscote, etc.

I have not seen John lately: he has been away but Papa B. & Tom seem flourishing.

This district is very quiet & good air abounds & it is very attainable by 'bus & rail & I think we shall like it very much. It was *necessary* for us to settle now for a time—the *event* is *expected* in August—*think of that*.

Do you interest yourself in Music now? If so I will sometime send you some new little capers of mine, which you can mock at & destroy.

My kindest regards to Mrs. Buck & Morton & with much affection

Yours ever sincerely,
Edward Elgar

Alice had the knack of making even a small house look distinctive. She spent a lot of time on detail—on the placing of furniture, on table decoration, on flower arrangements, and so on. She was no cook, but employed servants—the experienced Sarah Allen and a Mrs. Gough—who were expert in this science. But she knew what refinements impressed visitors. For instance, if one called at the right time, there was the possibility that one would be offered Turkish coffee in handleless cups. And visitors did begin to appear. The Townshends (who were now living at Hill Fields, Redmarley, to whose church they had presented a long kneeler for the altar step in 1888) came to dinner on 16 May. A fortnight later Mrs. Fitton was a luncheon guest, while Lady Montgomery, a formidable widow of Sir Robert Montgomery of Indian Army fame, called during the afternoon.

On 14 August—a week late—a daughter was born to Alice. By now the new overture *Froissart* had been accepted for performance at the Worcester Festival and for publication by Novello. At this cheerful time the Bucks were welcome visitors, and a week before setting off for Worcester Elgar wrote to Buck.

West Kensington.
Aug 31:
1890

The original MS of Clapham Town[5] end is enclosed for depositure in the Settle Museum.

My dear Charles,

First we hope you are all right & you both had a nice journey home & found all well—*except the patients* I ought to add.

Now, *if you can* do send me a line telling me what is a 'Materia Medica'? 'Cos why?

'Cos our nurse has been very good & wants one, and we thought we should like to give it to her as a surprise. Now I know it's a book; but it is *one* book or *several*, or are there many editions, or can any ass make a list of physic stuffs & call it that: in the multitude of counsellors is there desperation—to the lay mind.

Now there's a dear, quiet, docile Charles, pr'y thee, put thy quaint pen to virgin paper—not a p.c. please or they will read your screed—& tell me what is the one to get for a professional person, price & etc. etc.

[5] See reproduction of this MS. in *Elgar O.M.* facing p. 128.

> . . . I thought to enforce my appeal by beginning like the Sailor's prayer—*'Lord! I don't trouble ye often!'* but I know you will not mind.
>
> All is going on well here & I have been promoted to nurse my offspring—a fearful joy & fatal to trousers . . . I wd. as soon nurse an *'automatic irrigator'*. But it's a pretty little thing.
>
> Love to all,
> Ever yours
> Edward Elgar.

The child was baptised on 2 September, Miss Gully, its nurse only consenting to attend the Catholic ceremony provided she did not have to bow down to any images. Derived from CAR—as in C. A. Roberts—or from Caroline, plus the termination of Alice, and previously used in the dedication of *Liebesgrüss*, the name Carice was bestowed on the infant, together with Irene. After the success of *Froissart* at Worcester Edward was joined by wife and daughter for a holiday. They stayed with the Townshends and went around Redmarley, and then with the Whinfields, at Severn Grange, in Worcester. In December the Elgars were back again in the Midlands, as guests of Mary Baker, who was then living at Covertside, near Hasfield. Edward was already teaching some pupils in Malvern[6] on a regular basis, and after Christmas he found it necessary to increase his teaching load there, as nothing seemed to be moving particularly fast on the London front. In the early part of 1891 Elgar was in Malvern from Tuesday to Thursday, sometimes even to Friday, and it became clear that the sensible thing to do was to cut losses and retire to the provinces. In a depressing period Edward and Alice subscribed to a series of *The Hundred Best Pictures*, published by Charles Letts & Co.,[7] and made their own Index.

The house in Avonmore Road was disposed of, and after seeing a number of properties rented one in Alexandra Road.

[6] Haynes & Co., Musical Instrument Merchants, conducted their business in the Cecilia Hall, where teaching rooms were available for hire. Mr. W. Haynes was organist at the Priory Church.

[7] This was published fortnightly, each part with six reproductions. Carice Elgar Blake wrote of a periodical "published monthly, with twelve reproductions".

This was named "Forli", after the painter Melozzo da Forli who came from a town of that name not far from Ravenna. The Elgars moved in on 20 June. Edward then spent a good deal of time playing chamber music at the Fittons, but he also spent a fair amount of time ill in bed. He was, indeed, very low at times, with his eyes, his throat and his teeth all causing trouble in turn. And when he had recovered from these afflictions he fell victim to influenza at the beginning of 1892. Alice sold off Hazeldine furniture that she didn't want, and what she did want was moved into "Forli".

Here Alice began to adjust to realities of semi-detachment and relative penury. On 25 March Hazeldine was finally disposed of and with their joint incomes (in the case of Alice unearned) the Elgars made a brave show of keeping up with the Fittons, Fletchers, Sharpes, and all those who gathered together to play or to listen to the new music—especially Brahms and Grieg. There was something of an œcumenical atmosphere at "Forli" on occasion, with the Fathers Coldwell and Keiren, from the Catholic Church, and Capel-Cure, as frequent visitors. On 19 June Alice's Aunt Emma Raikes, having sent for her brother Robert and her sister Caroline to be at her deathbed, died. She was buried in Longhope churchyard.

The Bakers maintained their lively interest in the doings of the Elgars and in the summer of 1892 Mary Frances Baker made possible a German holiday for them, which made a profound impression. It was a time when Anglo–German relations were at their best, with both countries prepared, as Gladstone said, to execute "the great purposes of providence for the advantage of mankind", which meant dividing up the world into profitable spheres of influence. Elgar himself had spent a decade in reflection on those ways of Providence which had bestowed such musical benefits on the German people as he had seen on his sole previous visit to Germany.

Before leaving for the Continent he left completed vocal scores of *The Black Knight* and *Spanish Serenade* with Novellos. Acceptance of these works following on the appearance of *Froissart* from the same firm was heartening. Back home from Germany Alice and Edward settled down to work with renewed vigour. Alice saw herself in a new role. Certainly she was the helpmeet of her husband—according to principles to which she had been accustomed from her now vanished youth—but she was also the intellectual wing of the Roberts–Elgar song combine. From 22 August there was a concentrated week of joint effort. Edward was "fired with songs", with "A Spear, a Sword", of which the text is no longer extant, and of "1588". What Miss Simpson—who sang some of the songs on 26 August, the day when the letter was written—thought is not related. No doubt the valiant residents of Malvern found its sentiments much to their taste. As for Alice herself it is clear that the aspirations she had entertained in youth in respect of a more radical society had been submerged beneath the weight of family tradition and the infection of patriotism that was rife in the so-called Age of Armed Peace. At the foot of "1588" Alice wrote: "For my Beloved's booful music". Provokingly she also wrote: "Pease [*sic*] not beat. Will dis do?"

Loose, loose the sails, the anchor slip,
The moon rides high, the clouds fly fast;
Pass on the cup from lip to lip
Perchance it is the last, the last
That we may quaff ere life be past;
Quaff on and arm.

The grim, great galleon rests tonight
And heaves with every surging wave,
A moment more she'll be in sight,
A moment more the sea may rave
O'er you and me in storm-tost grave;
No eye to heed.

But sword in hand we'll board the foe,
And shouting loud old England's name
We'll storm their deck with thrust and blow,
Then welcome death or life the same
For dearer far than life is Fame;
On, comrades, on!

After a week of song-writing Edward turned to the orchestration of *The Black Knight*, and Alice to the supervision of the men who came to put a new fire-grate in the drawing-room. She also had to comfort Edward when, on 7 September, Scap, the collie brought back from Yorkshire in 1885, died. On 26 September *The Black Knight* was complete. "May all good be with his booful Music", was Alice's fervent hope. Edward meanwhile was teaching the girls at Cambridge House, at Miss Fletcher's school, at the High School in Worcester, as well as the other pupils accommodated above Haynes's shop in Malvern. At the beginning of December he went back to his desk and found two poems of which the poet was under some obligation to Wilhelm Müller and his *Schöne Müllerin.* On the second piece Alice wrote: "In case my Beloved might like it".

THE MILL WHEEL

I. *Winter*

On and on the water flows
   Stops the mill wheel never,
Crashing on and on it goes
   Hearts may ache for ever.

Once it sounded joyously
   Hearing it together,
All the birds sang merrily
   Bees hummed in the heather.

Then we stood and watched the spray
   Watched the rainbow quiver,
Gone is sunshine, past is May;
   Dreary rushes shiver.

Touch of hand is but a dream,
   All Love's gift is hidden,
Sweetest eyes no more may gleam
   Sorrow comes unbidden.

II. *May*

(A Rhapsody)

Oh! the rush of the water free
Oh! the hum of the joyous bee,
Oh! the singing of birds in May,
And blue of the sky today.

For it's oh! my own love is here
While the mill wheel is crashing near,
And the blossoms and buds arise
And welcome their sister eyes.

And I've touched both her hand and brow
Oh! the mill wheel may thunder now,
Let it splash, let it dash at will
Our hearts' song is louder still.

Against the third line of the first stanza Edward wrote in one draft "vessy nice"!

In 1893 Edward's *Spanish Serenade* and *The Black Knight* were given their first performances, in Hereford and Worcester respectively. Composer and poet went for walks in the fields, or in Birchwood, and they looked for the first signs of spring and the coming of swallow and cuckoo. Maybe this was not quite the life of Eveline in *The Portrait*, nor of Olive in *Marchcroft Manor*, but it was not unrewarding. It was creative and productive, and in the imagery of Alice's latest verses the thrill of passion is not disguised. The summer was made exciting by the festivities that attended the engagement of the Duke of York to Princess May of Teck—and Alice no doubt was inspired by the fact that in honour of the Imperial Jubilee, three Rajahs and detachments of Indian soldiery took part in the processions in London.

8
The "Bavarians"

There was hardly a school for girls in that much schooled town of Malvern in which Elgar did not teach. The one which came to assume a place of special prominence in the life of the Elgars was The Mount, over which a Miss Rosa Burley—a musical lady who played the violin—now presided.

Prior to being received into the Roman Catholic Church (which took place during the year 1893–4) Alice went to The Mount to take instruction in Latin. Between Miss Burley and the Elgars there was a common interest in Germany, and in 1893 it appeared that Miss Burley would be in Germany, with a pupil—Alice Davey—at the same time as the Elgars. So it was agreed that since Miss Burley was having to deal with accommodation anyway she should undertake also to find rooms in Munich for the Elgars.

On 20 July Miss Burley reported to Alice on the arrangements so far made. Four days later she dined at "Forli". The house was to have been let for the summer holiday, but this plan fell through, and the Elgars were left with the problem of what to do with the infant Carice. In the end Mary Frances Baker nobly came to the rescue and took the child off her parents' hands. The family plate was packed into a chest, and the chest was deposited with Basil Nevinson. On 2 August all was in order and Alice and Edward duly set off for Bavaria.

Concerning the visit Miss Burley left some rough notes.

> Miss B. I am longing to hear more Operas—I know so little of Wagners music—and do want to know more about it. I heard the Siegfried Idyll when they first performed it at S. James's Hall, under Richter and I thought it was lovely.
>
> Elgar—I heard that too. I went up from Worcester & came back in the middle of the night by the Fish and Milk train from Paddington where are you going to stay?
>
> Miss B.—I don't know yet but 'Fräulein' is writing for all sorts

of addresses of rooms and it seems quite easy & they are very cheap.

Elgar—Everyone stays at the 'bier Jahresgarten'—but that is very expensive.

Regenten—We hear the Ring [August 20, 21, 23, 25], Lohengrin [not noted by Elgar], Tristan and Isolde [also not noted by Elgar], Flying Dutchman [not noted by Elgar]. [The Elgars saw *The Mastersingers* with Miss Burley on 17 August, and *Die Feen* on 27 August, while Miss Burley was with them for the *Tannhäuser* performance on 24 August]. Levi conducted.

Munich was lovely. We had meals in Restaurants & Bier Gardens, we ate sausages in Hans Sachs Mrs. Elgar ecstatically casting her eyes upward—"What a darling old man he was"!

Elgar—"Yes! but I expect he blew his nose with his fingers".

Mrs. E—inexpressibly shocked—"Oh Edu—we won't dwell on that".

We heard excellent music in the Biergartens—Hofbräukeller—suppers—Wiener Schnitzel in the Rathauskeller.

Elgar was unrecognisable. He expanded, laughed and enjoyed himself.

He took extensive notes and worked hard. Very often Alice Davey and I wanted him to come out & play but his wife would not let him very wisely no doubt.

We went about in the little horse trams. They ran till midnight, and we were sorry for the poor old weary horses.

We went to the Starnberger See with its lovely panorama of the snow covered mountains. Sometimes Elgar would say "Oh! think of Malvern", and we all sighed and groaned at the thought of going back to the stiffness and convention.

We all went to Garmisch and heard the Tyrolese players doing the Schuplättl Dances in the Drei Möhren.[1]

Elgar's Bavarian Dances were suggested by this—They are very charming and expressing perfectly the feeling of the Tyrolese music.

This visit to Munich had an important effect upon Elgar.

The Elgars visited Bavaria again in 1894 and yet again in 1895, both times Carice being left with Miss Burley. Meanwhile Edward's career was positively taking shape, and his name as composer in wider circulation. *The Black Knight* was duly published and performed, and among other projects *King Olaf* was emerging as a major enterprise. On 6 February 1895 Alice

[1] See *The Record of a Friendship*, 1972, p. 71: the Elgars were not present on this occasion; they had been in Garmisch before going to Munich to join Miss Burley and Alice Davey.

"heard lovely news of part songs 'Snow' and 'Singing bird'—very happy". It was a long time since those gentle word pictures had appeared as interludes in *Isabel Trevithoe*. Their reissue in Edward's sympathetic settings was a new consummation of a marriage of souls; and Novello paid twelve guineas for them.

Elgar's creativity was stirred by scenes, by pictures, by books. Sometimes there was a conjunction of circumstances that acted as stimulus. So it was in respect of the "Bavarians".

At that period anything relating to the principal romantic holiday and tourist centres of Europe was meet for exploitation by artists in search of ideas acceptable to a middle-class public. Just as Spain was represented in the painter's (and Elgar's) repertoire so too was Bavaria. No artist made a better job of Bavarian themes than Bavarian-born Hubert von Herkomer (1849–1914), who had been brought to England as a child, had become a much sought-after portrait and landscape painter, and was naturalised in 1907. He was keenly musical (there are interesting musical references in his lectures) and painted portraits of, among others, Wagner, Brahms, Joachim, Hallé, and Stanford. His works always attracted attention at the Grosvenor Gallery—where the exhibitions gave much pleasure to Alice, and was equally at home in oils or water-colours. In the latter medium his *tour de force* was acknowledged to be *Light, Life, and Melody*, first exhibited in 1879, of which Henry Blackburn wrote in the Illustrated Catalogue:

> The scene is in the Bavarian Highlands, where peasants are assembled in the evening in the bowling alley of a mountain *Bierhaus*, listening to a visitor playing on their national instrument, the zither.
>
> This picture is not only interesting to us technically, as an experiment in water-colour, but also as an exact rendering of the *couleur locale*. . . .

Herkomer also showed that year his *Auf der Alm*, a study of Bavarian women at work in the mountain pastures. In 1882 Herkomer's powerful study of the head of his father Lorenz, a Bavarian wood-carver, was soon in the Grosvenor Gallery Summer Exhibition, and in 1883 *Words of Comfort*—an old woman and a girl seated under the eaves of a Bavarian chalet—of which an etching appeared also in *The Magazine of Art*.

Alice Elgar was susceptible to pictures and behind her Bavarian experiences of the 1890's lay Herkomer's reflections of Bavarian life. As a matter of fact the rigours of that life, insofar as they affected the tourist, caused her some trepidation. She had no head for heights and nothing she disliked more than crossing a mountain stream on a wooden bridge lacking a handrail! However, the scenic beauty impressed her deeply, as also Edward. The songs which emerged from this set of experiences have a quality of inward joyfulness that bespeaks a compatibility over and above that usually allowed to have existed within the Elgars' marital relationship. It is a physical alertness that keeps the songs alive, and this quality is from within and not merely reactive to the supposed nature of Bavarian popular music.

Alice and Edward worked together on these pieces and the process of verbal sublimation was a long one. The development of the text of the songs may be traced through various extant drafts that bear marks of frequent revision and annotation by each partner. The aim was to provide a vehicle for music, and the several attempts at shaping and re-shaping show clearly how the search for workable rhythmic patterns and for phrase continuity proceeded. It is not possible to place all the drafts of pieces in chronological order with absolute certainty, but the manner in which words move towards finality may be inferred from the alterations and modifications.

The final, authentic texts of all the songs were copied by Alice on to the staveless reverse of cut-down sheets of music manuscript paper, headed

> Words for six Bavarian Partsongs
> for Chorus and Orchestra
> Music by Edward Elgar.

There was also on the title-page this inscription:

> To E. E.
> from C. A. E. 5 March 1895

On 25 March Edward played the songs as they then had been composed to Isabel Fitton and her sister Hilda Capel-Cure, and on 9 April they were noted as "finished". On 12 December negotiations for publication were concluded with Joseph

Williams. The first performance of the "dear Bavarians"—as Alice called them—was in Worcester on 21 April 1896.

The Bavarian poems were centred on Garmisch-Partenkirchen, two adjoining villages (brought together under one administration) lying below the Zugspitze—at 2,963 metres the highest peak of the German–Austrian Alps. In due course Garmisch became celebrated because Richard Strauss lived here for a great part of his life. Each of the Elgar pieces commemorates some particular place in the vicinity of Garmisch, although it is not always quite clear which refers to what!

The initial inspiration for the project would appear to have come from Edward. On the unstaved reverse of one sheet of music manuscript paper are to be found these rhythmic patterns as belonging in due course to the first two of the Bavarians. Words cancelled are shown in square brackets.

From here consideration passes to the existing versions in Alice's manuscripts. These are respectively identified from A–M. As in the previous cases cancelled words, or phrases, are shown within square brackets, while annotations and other marginal matter are given in italics.

(1) A In pencil, on the reverse of a half sheet of notice to the Ladies' (Orch[estra, Worcester]; right hand half of paper only. The front of the notice has

Come away to dance come away

The reverse lists these poems:

No. 1 The Dance
No. 2 Aspiration
No. 3 Lullaby
No. 4 False Love
No. 5 The Marksman

Come, the dance now calls us away,
will do
Haste, the fiddles & fifes now play;
Hark; what joyous sounds!
Come & dance a merry measure
Quaff the bright brown ale my treasure
Ha! my heart upbounds!

II

Slow

p Great was the world before the flood:
mf Great was the flood that [indecipherable deletion] wet the world:
ff Great was the flood that wet the world
fishes! †
And upset all the men!
[deletion]
sun———
(all long) O! how *lovely* is the
sunshine.
sun———†
O! how lovely is the sunshine.
Great was the world before the flood etc. etc.

I

Quick (mässig)

(short) How I love to hear the music
† How I love to hear the music
(a) Sounding from so far!
far! far! (if possible a single syllable)

How I love to hear the music
† How I love to hear the music
(a) Sounding out so loud!
loud! loud!

---

† pencil

ff Come, come and join in the dance,
† (*b*) Come, come and join in the dance,

† Dancing is so joy ous
(b) Come, come, and join in the dance
come come and join in the dance
Dancing is so joy-ful!
[Joy! joy! joy!]
so! so! so!
D. C. How I love etc.

(a) (b) new
(a) Same? (a) as before
(b) (*a*) † to end

II

Slow.

p Great was the world before the flood:
mf Great was the flood that wet the world:
f Great was the flood that wet the world
And upset all the fishes!

—

(long) O! how lovely is the sun shine.
O! how lovely is the sun shine.

—

Great was the world before the flood
&c. &c.

I

Quick. (missing)

How I love to hear the music
How I love to hear the music
(a) Sounding from so far!
far! far! (if possible a single syllable)

How I love to hear the music
How I love to hear the music
(a) Sounding out so loud!
loud! loud!

—

(b) A. Come, come and join in the dance,
Come, come and join in the dance,
Dancing is so joy-ous
(b) Come come and join in the dance
come come and join in the dance
Dancing is so joy-ful!
~~Joy! joy! joy~~
so! so! so!

(a)
(a) Slow!
(b)
(b) well
D.C. How I love &c

(a
a) as before
to words.

Otherwise, in Elgar's hand, are suggestions towards *Lullaby* (No. 3) and *The Marksman* (No. 6) on a single sheet of writing paper in ink on recto and verso respectively:

p Softly rocking
moves the cradle
Mother sings to
Kleines kind:
Far away the
sounds of [dancing] music
[come] rise and tell us
[Of . . . joy] others joy
Mother will stay a home
[Nurse our] Rock & love little one
Music will ne'er beguile
Mother will sing to thee
Hush thee & croon to thee
Ever be good to thee
Sleep oh sleep [my child] on my bosom

as at first
Softly rocking
moves the cradle
Mother sings to
Kleine [*sic*] Kind
Far away the
sounds of music
rise & tell us
[dance]
others joy.

IV quick
Come! see the shooters shoot — . . — . .
See! how we *stand* & fire — . . — . .
Fire at the target gay — . . — . .
Hitting each time! — . . ——
See all the garlands glad
Wreaths are for marksmen good
Bullets ne'er miss their mark
Here in the wood!
Come! come! see how the shooters shoot.

Softly rocking
moves the cradle
Mother sings to
Kleinste Kind:
Far away the
sound of ~~[illegible]~~ music
~~came~~ rise and tell us
~~of [illegible] joy.~~
others' joy.

or, at first
Softly rocking
moves the cradle
Mother sings to
Kleinste Kind
Far away the
sounds of music
rise & tell us
others' ~~[illegible]~~ joy.

Mother will sing a hymn
Look & love
~~[illegible]~~ little one
Dancing must & wait awhile
Music will [illegible] beguile
Mother will sing to thee
Hush thee & sleep & be
Ever be good to thee
Sleep on ~~[illegible]~~ sleep
on my bosom

IV.

Come! see the ~~shortening~~ shot
Ten! how we strive to fire
Five! at the target firing
Hitting each time!
See all the garlands flame
Wreaths are for marksmen proud
Bullets now win their meed
Here in the wood!
Come! see! see how the shortening shot

B In pencil on the reverse of a quarter-sheet of music MS. paper.

No. 1
Come, the dance calls us away
Haste, the fife and fiddles play
Hark what joyous sounds!

Come and dance a merry measure
Quaff the bright brown ale my treasure
Ha! my heart upbounds.

C In ink on the reverse of a quarter-sheet of music MS. paper

No. 1 *Zu [m] r Zugspitze-Garmisch*

1

Come away, the dance awaits us,
Merry eyes will glance and greet us. x
Hark! what joyous sounds!
Let us drink and dance my treasure,
Quaff the bright brown ale at pleasure, x
Ha! my heart upbounds!

2

Sweet heart come, on let us haste,
On, on, no [moment to] time let us waste.
With my heart I love thee!
Dance, dance, for rest we disdain,
Turn, twirl, and spin round again,
With my arm I hold thee!

3

Down the path the lights are gleaming
Friendly faces gladly beaming,
Welcome us with song.
Dancing makes the heart grow lighter,
Makes the world and life grow brighter
Come dance along!

D In ink, on the reverse of a half-sheet of music MS. paper, with numerous alterations and alternatives in pencil over text and in margin.

No. 1 *Zugspitze*
Zum Husaren
[Graseck[2]*]*

1 *Garmisch*

Come and hasten to the dancing
Merry eyes will soon be glancing,
Hark ! what joyous sounds !
[Full of mirth we'll dance & gaily,
Wishing pleasure could come daily !]
Let us dance & drink at pleasure
Quaffing bright brown ale at leisure

2

Sweet heart haste, [though not to rest]
Turn, (twirl, and [spring with the best,]
With my arm I hold thee !
Haste, haste, far onwards we'll fare
Dance, dance, and banish all care
With my heart I love thee !

3

Down the path the lights are gleaming
Friendly faces gladly beaming
[With a joyous] Welcome us with song,
Dancing makes the heart grow lighter
Makes the world and life grow brighter
As we dance along.

[Haste &] Come away
the dance awaits us
Come away to the dancing(?)
Merry eyes [are glad to] will glance
& greet us
Let us drink & dance my treasure
Quaffing brown bright ale at pleasure.
soon we'll begin soon we'll begin merrily
round again spin Turn & twirl & [round]
Come [haste] spin around
Sweet heart rest . . .
Turn & Twirl spin round
let's
to no
Dance dance
not
[To the dance]
Sweet heart come . . .
On, on, no . . .
With my
Dance
[Come]
Turn . . .

E In ink, on the reverse of a half-sheet of music MS. paper

No. 1 *Zum Zugspitze* *Garmisch*

Come and hasten to the dancing,
Merry eyes will soon be glancing,
Hark ! what joyous sounds !

[2] Graseck is SE. of Garmisch, some six or seven kilometres from the Zugspitze.

Let us drink and dance, my treasure,
Quaf[fing bright brown] the† foaming† ale at pleasure,
    Ha ! my heart upbounds !

Sweetheart haste, soon we 'll begin
Turn, [and] twirl, & round [ever again] spin   *lightly*†
    With my [arm around thee] heart I love thee !
Haste haste, for onwards we' ll fare
    Dance, dance [and banish dull] forgetting our care
    With my arm I'll hold thee !   *D. C.*†

Down the path the lights are gleaming,
Friendly faces gladly beaming,
    Welcome us with song.
Dancing makes the heart grow lighter,
Makes the world and life grow brighter,
    As we dance along !

F Final version in ink on reverse of quarter sheets of MS. paper. Title page as shown above on p. 120; contents on reverse of title page

		numbering above the poems
No. 1	The Dance	No. 1
2	Aspiration	No. 4
3	Lullaby	No. 3
4	False Love	No. 2
5	The Marksman	No. 6
6	True Love	No. 5

Leutasch Thal, deleted below, is across the Austrian frontier, some way south of Garmisch. Sonnenbichl, on the other hand, is on the northern side of and near to Garmisch.

No. 1   [Im Leutasch Thal]
The Dance
Sonnenbichl

Come and hasten to the dancing,
Merry eyes will soon be glancing,
    Ha ! my heart upbounds.
Come and dance a merry measure,
Quaff the bright brown ale my treasure,
    Hark ! what joyous sounds

2

Sweetheart come, on let us haste,
On, on, no time let us waste,
With my heart I love thee!
Dance, dance, for rest we disdain *p. 14 treasure?*
Turn, twirl, and spin round again,
With my arm I hold thee!

3

Down the path the lights are gleaming
Friendly faces gladly beaming
Welcome us with song.
Dancing makes the heart grow lighter
Makes the world and life grow brighter
As we dance along!

G In pencil, on sheet of plain paper

1

Now we hear the Spring's sweet voice
Singing gladly through the world,
Bidding all the earth rejoice.

2

All is merry in the field,
Flowers blossom in the grass,
Blossoms blue, red, white they yield.

3

[When] As I seek my sweetheart true
Sings the little lark on high
Fain to send her praises due.

4

And I climb [before] & reach her door
Ah! I see a rival there,
Ah! fare well for ever more—

5

Ever true was I to thee
Never grieved or vexed thee, love,
False, oh false art thou to me

6

Now out in the forest green
Far from cruel eyes that mock
Will I dwell, unloved, unseen

Wamberg is a village to the west of Garmisch

F

No. 2 *Wamberg*
False Love

1.
Now we hear the spring's sweet voice
Singing gladly through the world
Bidding all the earth rejoice.

2.
All is merry in the field,
Flowers [blossom] grow amidst† in the grass
? Blossoms blue, red, white they yield

3.
maiden†
As I seek my *sweetheart* true,
Sings the little lark on high
[Fain] [Glad] to send her praises due

[4] 2
As I climb and reach her door,
Ah ! I see a rival there,
So? [Ah !] [Now] farewell for evermore

5
Ever true was I to thee,
Never grieved or vexed thee, love,
False, oh ! false, art thou to me.

6
Now amid the forest green,
? Far from *cruel eyes that mock,*
? Will I dwell unloved, unseen—

H On same kind and size of paper as F, variants only shown below.

No. 4 *Wamberg*

Stanza 2/2
Flowers blossom in the grass

stanza 3/1
As I seek my sweet heart true

3/3
Fain to send her praises due

stanza 4/3
Ah ! farewell for everymore !
stanza 6 wanting.

Hammersbach is south of Garmisch

1(a) In pencil, on plain sheet of paper

No. 3
Sleep my [little one, sleep] son oh slumber softly
While thy mother watches by thee
Nothing can afright or harm thee
Sleep my [little] son, [sleep] oh slumber softly.

Far away
Zithers play;
Dancing gay
Calls today.

Vainly play
Zithers gay
Here I stay
All the day

Happily
Peacefully
Guarding thee
Watching thee.

On reverse, all cancelled.

(b) Sleep my little son sleep softly
While thy mother [*illegible*] watches by thee
Nothing can awake or harm thee
Sleep my little son sleep softly,
While mother sings thy lullaby

Sleep my little son sleep softly
While thy mother watches by thee
Nothing can affright or harm thee
Sleep my little son sleep softly

Far away . . . [as (*a*)]
. . .
Happily
Peacefully watching thee, guarding thee.

F

No. 3 *Bei Hammersbach*
Lullaby

Sleep my son, O slumber softly!
While thy mother watches [by] o'er thee
(C) *again* Nothing can affright or harm thee
rhyme (E)
Sleep [my son, O slumber softly] Oh sleep! my son.

Far away . . . as I (a)
. . .
Happily
Guarding thee
Peacefully
Watching thee

Up a pinewood path behind Partenkirchen is the pilgrims' chapel, with a pink and white cupola, and a silver and pink interior, built in 1734

J In ink, on half-sheet of plain paper

No. 2 *Sanct Anton*
Over the height[s] the snow lies deep
Sunk is the land in [dreamy] peaceful sleep;
Here, by the house of God we pray
Lead, Lord, our souls today.

Shielding, like the silent snow
Fall God's mercies here below.

Calmly then like the snow bound land
Rest we in His protecting Hand;
Bowing, we wait His mighty will.
Lead, Lord, and guide us still.

F

No. [2] 4 *Bei Sanct Anton*
Aspiration

Only variants from J
line 6 Fall His . . .
,, 9 . . . Will

The published version of the next song *On the Alm* is also qualified by *Hoch Alp*. *Hoch Alp* designates a "High Alp" and this one is located south of Hammersbach. An *Alm* was a pasture in the mountains, where there would be a hut in which a peasant girl—a *Sennerin*—would live during the summer to tend the cows. This was thought to be a picturesque and romantic way of life and attracted the attention of poets, musicians, and painters (see Herkomer).

K In ink on plain sheet of paper.

On the Alm [added in pencil]
A [pretty] mellow bell [rings] peals near
It has so sweet a sound,
I know a maiden dear
With voice as full and round
A sun[ny] lit Alm shines clear
With clover blossoms sweet,
There dwells my maiden dear
And there my love I meet.

[And] [Then] There flying with no fear
The swallows pass all day;
And fast, my maiden dear
Sees chamois haste away.
I cannot stay wait, down† here
I cannot stay wait† below;
To seek my maiden dear
I, on the Alm, must go.

The mountain's call I hear,
And up the heights I bound;
I knew my maiden dear
Would [hear] mark my
sound.

Rejoicing come I here
My flaxen haired sweetheart;
I love thee maiden dear—Nay! bid me not depart!

F Variants on K

No. [6] 5 *On the Alm*
True Love

Stanza 2/3
[There] *Where* pencil alteration

2/4
And I [there] my love [I] may meet. pencil alterations

4/1
I cannot [wait down] linger here corrections

4/4
I [on] to from this point in red ink

5/3
I [knew] know

5/4
[Would] Will
scene of the

The last of the published set, *The Marksman*, is Murnau on the Staffelsee, and here we are brought into the activity of the Shooting Club and, indeed, the atmosphere of *Der Freischütz*.

L In pencil on plain paper

No. 5

1
The Sun is sinking in the west
And lights the peaks with crimson glow,
Now shadow fills the vale with rest
And stars look peace on all below.

2
our joy's best crown
And love will give
us praises sweet
As homewards now our [*illegible*] way we take
For crowned we come with praises meet
Which dearer seem for love's [*illegible*] dear sake.

we'll win with such
And love
will greet our fresh renown
For homewards now [our way we take] we take our way
And love will be our joy's best crown
[And] The best of [the] prizes won today

F No. [5] 6 *The Marksman*

[1]
Come from the mountain side,
Come from the valleys wide,
See how we muster strong
Tramping along!

[2]
Rifle[s] on shoulder sling,
Powder and bullets bring,
Manly in mind and heart,
Play we our part.

[3]
Sure be each eye today,
Steady each hand must stay,
If in the trial we
Victors would be! < [crescendo mark in red ink]

4
Sharp is the crack! [it's] 'tis done!
Lost is the chance, or won;
Right in the gold is it?
Huzza! the hit!—

5
The sun [is sinking in] will sink [soon] & light† the west
And [light[s]] touch the peaks with crimson glow;
[Now] [And] Then shadows fill[s] the vale with rest
[And] While stars look peace on all below.

6
In triumph [now] then we take our way
And with our prizes homeward wend;
Through meadows sweet with new mown hay
A song exultant will we send.

7
Oh! love will smile at such renown
And [surely] give us praises [glad will say] meet and dear
Such joy will be our life's best crown,
The best of prizes won [today this year.]
First 4 verses *da capo*

There are three further fragments which relate to the "Bavarians". The first, on a page from an exercise book, is a sketch in sonnet form as for *Aspiration*. But the occasion was not a visit to St. Anton's Chapel, but to the Kitzbühler Horn, in the Austrian Alps.

M In pencil
On the Kitzbuhler [*sic*] Horn
Nought broke the *summer* silence of the [circles] height[s]
In solemn circle vast
Vast & hung [with]   their eternal crown of snow,
We [stood &] saw
And all the world looked small [& shrunk] & dwarfed below
Our souls were awed
spirits rapt to see such—[such] and [lights] sight
[As] [Which lay among the clefts] of rockbound might
Within the narrow Chapel wall [. . . built] the Crucified
Looked down & all our life seemed sanctified
Anew to reach to higher things & purer light.
Then my belovèd placed his hand in mine   1
And said, 'Whatever love I gave to thee   2
What fealty I gave thee O my wife   3
Thy thoughts, thy touch more closer entertwine   1
My being every day [entirely] perfectly   †   2
Our souls, God grant in death & life.   3

Songs from the Bavarian Highlands represents the end of a chapter in the life of the Elgars, signifying a peak in personal fulfilment and mutual happiness, the consummation of the poetic fancy which had lived within Alice since girlhood. For poetry revealed through music is—or was in Alice's view—the perfection of sensible expression. Perhaps never again did the Elgars return to the pleasure in living and working together shown in this compilation of impressions of summer days in Bavaria.

The idea for a musico-poetic record of such times came when Edward was holding on to small gains in the campaign to establish himself as a composer. As the "Bavarians" came towards their first performances the name of Elgar commanded widening respect. He had arrived, and *Lux Christi* and *King Olaf* were on the point of doing so too.

And for Alice there was another cause for satisfaction.

10 Sheffield Gardens
Campden Hill W
28 June 1895

Dear Madam:

The Editor of the Dictionary of National Biography has asked me to write a notice of the late Sir Henry Gee Roberts, and has sent me the materials you have been kind enough to furnish. May I venture to ask if you can give me information on the following points:

1) the exact date & place of birth.
2) the name of his mother and of her father.
3) the regiment to which he was posted on arrival in India.
4) the date of his marriage.
5) how many sons & daughters survived him.

Yours very truly
E. M. Lloyd

On 9 July Lloyd wrote again:

Dear Madam:

I am much obliged for your letter & its enclosures. It is seldom that one is able to obtain such complete information as you have kindly furnished.

I will take care to return you all the papers.

Yours very truly
E. M. Lloyd

A little more than a year later Alice went into the London Library to read the memoir of her father in *The Dictionary of National Biography*. A future qualifier for inclusion in a supplement to that publication was at the time negotiating with Manns for a Crystal Palace performance of *King Olaf*.

9

Child Welfare in the Victorian Era

The Elgars were neither the first nor the last married couple, with interests outside and problems within the household, to discover that a small child could present particular difficulties. There was the need to find someone to look after Carice when her parents were away, and when they were at home it was a requirement that she should be inconspicuous during her father's working hours. In the end a common solution to both problems was discovered; but this brought other complications in its train.

When she was three Carice was entertained during her parents' absence in Bavaria by Mary Frances Baker, whose house was a fairly frequent calling place during her infancy. Apart from the fact that "it always seemed to be lovely weather there" Carice remembered the fascination afforded by Miss Baker's breakfast-time coffee-making ritual. Sometimes Carice was left with the eccentric Aunt Vee at Hill Ash, where she sat enthralled at the sight of this hypochondriacal lady washing her money. Alice remained a victim of the tradition of afternoon visiting to which she had been accustomed from youth, and as she was determined that Carice should inherit the accepted courtesies took her with her whenever it was not inconvenient. The little girl sat, and usually suffered, as her elders talked above her disciplined silences. The Rileys, who lived at Putley Court, near Ledbury, were a particularly formidable prospect. Very grand and rather affected (there was a large family and all carrying carefully selected, and embarrassing, Anglo-Saxon names) they caused Carice to retire into her shell. With them in particular she felt painfully aware of her own shyness. When she went to Cheltenham, on the other hand, to visit two of her mother's old cousins—Grace and Agnes Probyn—she found a ready response to her own natural sense of curiosity. What she especially remembered was being given a pretty collection of jewellery to look at and to handle.

After her reception into the Catholic Church, like most converts Alice became fervent in the new faith—more so than her husband. Carice was given early instruction and most weeks, from as far back as she could remember, was taken to Mass. That she knew herself to be a Catholic posed problems whenever she went down into Raikes territory in Gloucestershire. In the churchyard at Dymock the tombs of various members of the family caused her at first to ask questions, and then, finding that they proved awkward for her elders, not to ask them.

However, so that the child could be the better able to discover facts for herself (as her mother had done in her girlhood) Alice insisted that Carice should learn to read at the earliest possible moment. She used to sit in the dining-room at "Forli" playing with her toys by the French window that opened out onto the garden. When free Alice would come and teach her her "letters". By the time she was four Carice was able to read. So far as reading was concerned it was what was read that decided social grading; with writing it was otherwise, it was how one wrote that counted. Or so Alice would say. She had "very rigid ideas of how a lady should hold a pen". Carice found her loyalties divided, and again, a crop of unaskable questions. Sometimes—though she had to cheat to be able actually to see him doing it—she watched her father at his desk, and she was horrified to notice that in his way of holding a pen there was no sign of observance of the required tenets of gentility.

With all the comings and goings Carice quickly acclimatised herself to the fact that her parents were people somewhat out of the ordinary. They spoke of strange things—like performances of *King Olaf* (to a rehearsal of which in Worcester she was taken when she was seven as a particular treat)—and distant places, like London and Bradford, and Wolverhampton. In this town a prominent place was occupied by the former Mary Frances Baker, who married Alfred Penny, the newly appointed Rector in 1895, who was a widower. Among the many visitors to "Forli" Carice remembered one who came particularly to see her mother rather than her father. Alice, a lady of letters, was delighted in 1896 to discover a more famous lady of letters staying in Malvern. This was Mrs. Eliza Lynn Linton (1822–98), the separated wife of W. J. Linton, the celebrated engraver, poet, and political reformer.

Mrs. Linton was novelist, essayist, and female liberationist. In her fictitious *Autobiography of Christopher Kirkland* (1885) she wrote her own life story. When Alice met her (and often entertained her at "Forli") she was working on a study of George Eliot which was published in 1897. How Alice came to terms with this lady with "advanced views" is not recorded; no doubt she found that they awakened earlier aspirations of her own.

In 1896 a more durable friendship began when Arthur Troyte Griffith, architect, first came to visit "Forli". His visits became a regular part of life, and apart from being a usual Sunday luncheon guest, he would drop in casually—even when Elgar was deeply involved. Troyte knew his place and was prepared to sit quietly in a corner of Elgar's little study as the orchestration of *King Olaf* proceeded apace. "Orchestration", wrote Troyte, "was a carefully organised business. Lady Elgar prepared the paper for the full score and he worked methodically doing ten or twelve pages a day". Troyte also had this to say:

> Elgar wanted absolute quiet when he was writing important music. At Forli he had a tent on the lawn where he was unapproachable and at Birchwood he could not be disturbed. He thought out his music before doing much writing, making notes of themes etc. When he began the Apostles, he saturated his mind with biblical literature. He was more absorbed in this than anything else written in Malvern. When he got well into it I had the kindest letter from his wife asking me not to call till it was finished as he wanted no distraction of any kind.[1]

But this is to anticipate. In 1897 Alice felt that "Forli" was not adequate and she began looking over other possible houses. In February Carice was left with the Acworths,[2] while her parents went up north. Next month she found herself spending

[1] MS notes by A. Troyte Griffith.

[2] Harry Dyke Acworth, a retired Indian Civil Servant, was a regular Pooh-Bah. He was Captain and Treasurer of the Golf Club and the Swimming Club, and President of the Ratepayers' Association and the Naturalists' Club in Malvern at various times. He also wrote the libretto for Elgar's *Caractacus*. He left Malvern, after 13 years in his various offices, in 1901.

a good deal of time at Birchwood, near Malvern, where the Elgars had rented a keeper's cottage.

> The cottage had several rooms and the well was immediately outside the front fence, and we drew the water—beautiful clear water—up in a large bucket. On one side of the cottage we walked straight into a lovely wood. In a tree close to the house Father had an elaborate system of traps for wasps and even hornets, which he looked after every day, putting fresh syrup and so on. We seem to have had an enormous number of wasps. Another great enjoyment here was the making of paths through the woods, and when I was at home, I was allowed to help, following [Father] and picking up the odd branches as he cut them off: my great delight was when there were quite a number of paths, and we used to set off, having arranged to take, for instance, two right turns and one left all the way, and see where we came out. I was always his 'man': he used to write me little notes . . . giving me instructions as to what I had to do the next day.[3]

For Carice these were idyllic days. And then the blow fell. Not only was she to go to school (she was now eight), she was to be a boarder. Even though she was to go to school in Malvern, home suddenly became thousands of miles away. But, reckoned Alice, if a genius—whether literary or musical—was to be served sacrifices had to be made. As for Carice, she reckoned the change would not be all that strange. She was to go to The Mount, and Rosa Burley, the proprietor, was quite a friend of the family.

Carice arrived at The Mount at the beginning of the summer term, and was put into a dormitory which she shared with three other little girls. Here she discovered how nasty little girls could be. Her companions thought that she had a funny name, and did not let her forget it. Her mother did not make life any easier. She insisted that out of doors Carice wore a red plush cape, with a lining of pale muslin material, whereas all the other girls had ordinary coats. She further was compelled to appear as an oddity by reason of the gold cross on a black velvet band which she had to carry round her neck. Nor was there much respite at the weekend. Alice called for her daughter each Sunday in time for Mass, after which they went home for the rest of the day. Alice then took the opportunity of supplementing

[3] MS notes by Carice Elgar Blake. For a "little note" See *Letters of Edward Elgar*, p. 70.

the instruction given at The Mount, and Carice was taken through sections of the Old Testament, given lines of poetry to learn by heart, heard to play her piano pieces, and rebuked for errors in deportment. Edward, however, provided some light relief. One of the trophies brought back from India by Uncle Stanley was a fox's head. Carice used to wonder where she would find it. Sometimes it was wrapped in a sheet and put in the bath. Sometimes it grinned down from the top of a wardrobe. All of which would seem to have added up to a curious kind of Sunday.

During that first summer at The Mount an old girlhood friend of Alice came to Malvern. Clementina Maxwell lived in some splendour at Munches near Dalbeattie, and proposed to the Elgars that she should take their small daughter back to Scotland for a holiday in which, no doubt, the child was at that time badly in need. Carice found the journey by overnight train exciting, and loved the freedom of the Scottish countryside, but wondered whether the morning prayers that were solemnly intoned each day had any kind of divine warrant.

The autumn was triumphant for Elgar. After the Gloucester festival, at which the "Meditation" from *Lux Christi* was played, came the first performance of *Caractacus* at Leeds, and after that the London premiere at the Crystal Palace. While all this was taking place Carice was busy contracting chicken-pox. It was the rule at The Mount that girls with infectious diseases should be removed until the danger of infecting the rest of the pupils was past. But since the Elgars were away when the illness was confirmed Miss Burley could only keep the child in moderate isolation in the school. At the beginning of 1899 there was another scare. The Elgar's maid, Mary, fell ill with scarlet fever. The girls from The Mount were still enjoying their Christmas holiday, so Carice was packed off there to be out of harm's way and under the care of the never-failing Miss Burley.

At last Alice found a house that she liked—one along the Wells Road that had lately been built and had a marvellous view across the plain to Bredon. Originally named "Congelow" it was designated by the anagrammatic Elgar "Craeglea". When she learned of this, Carice—already conscious of the fact that her name was the cause of a good deal of merriment—wondered what the girls were going to say when they heard what the new house was called. However, she had a little garden of her own, and found plenty of time to enjoy it. Indeed, she found too much time, for sometimes when told to stay there she felt miserably lonely. Once she had the temerity to say so to her mother. The answer was uncompromising. She must remember that she was the granddaughter of a general, and whenever grandfather had been told to stay in one place—no matter for how long—he stayed.

The summer of 1899 was one of great activity. Elgar, whose loyalty to the Sovereign was attested by the *Imperial March* and by the copy of *Caractacus* presented to (and graciously acknowledged by) the Queen, wrote a partsong in honour of her eightieth birthday. This led to a summons from Windsor to hear its performance. Later that year he was again at Windsor Castle for a concert at which a number of his pieces were performed. It was the year of the "Enigma" Variations, of *Sea Pictures*, and of preparations towards both *The Apostles* and *Gerontius*. At the beginning of June Carice developed whooping cough, was confined to her room under the care of Clementina Maxwell, who was now living in Cradley, in Worcestershire. While her father was being lionised in London Carice was repining at the doctor's refusal to allow her even to look out of the window during her illness.

The disciplines of childhood were various. Among them one of the more unpleasant was the cold bath. At Birchwood that summer Alice insisted that Carice underwent such purification, and she was required to prepare her own torture. She had to fetch water from the raintub outside the cottage, half fill the tub in her own room, and then step into the flotsam and jetsam that comprised a considerable part of the contents of the tub. There were those who sympathised with Carice's predicament. Among them in particular were the Misses Norbury, who lived at Sherridge, near Birchwood, and who used to invite Carice to play in their house and garden. Little things counted for much, and a coloured pin-cushion, with coloured pins, was a joy both then and in retrospect.

Those, nonetheless, were great days in Malvern, where for the élite among the inhabitants, contented in being in receipt of handsome private incomes, it was good to be alive, even if hypochondriacally so. In the summer there were Warner's Pair and the Four-Horse Brakes, and Char-a-Bancs, to provide an efficient service for sight-seeing, or if one wished to go further afield, there was the railway. In two hours one could be in Cheltenham, by way of Dymock, Newent, and Barber's Bridge. If one stayed at home a gentle constitutional as far as the Promenade Gardens allowed one to savour the delights of the Malvern Rhine String and Brass Band, directed by John Klee. In wintertime there were concerts by local talent; by the Musical Society, in the Church Institute at Malvern Link, by the Orchestral Society, or Mr. Lyon's Symphony Orchestra, in the Assembly Room, and by the Choral Society in the Wych School. Sometimes there were Grand Concerts, as when Clara Butt and Kennerley Rumford sang at the Assembly Room in the spring of 1899. There was opera too. The D'Oyly Carte Company played *The Mikado* in the Assembly Room in December 1899. In springtime, when the grounds of Madresfield House and the whole countryside was alive with new colour, Lady Mary Lygon conducted the Grand Concert during the Madresfield Musical Festival.

For those with other tastes, there were cricket, football, and golf; Trade Exhibitions, Mutoscope demonstrations, palmistry sessions, and Marvellous Marionettes. The young, with few opportunities to let their hair down, took their principal recreation during and after the Grand Confetti Fete.

When Carice was ten the old Queen died. This made a greater impression on her than had the first performance of *Gerontius* in Birmingham—which only led to tension and worry within the household—or her father's visit to Cambridge to receive an honorary degree were to do. She had been told by her mother that she was a lucky little girl to be living when a new century was dawning. She had also been taught that the Queen was a very special person deserving of all loyalty. Carice did not understand either proposition. What she did understand on 22 January 1901 was that the Queen was dead.

> I can remember Mother going out into the road to see if our neighbours had drawn their blinds. Unfortunately they had, so we were in a gloomy state with regard to light all day. We wore mourning. Mother got me a white blouse and a black skirt. As

she had always insisted on my having brown stockings, I had to wear them with the black skirt, which entirely spoilt the effect, and offended my dress sense.

The last five years of the nineteenth century was critical in the career of Elgar. As far as Alice was concerned she recognised a subtle change in her role. Certainly she felt that she should continue to exercise a cultural influence and her own career as a writer, even though her ideas were as likely as not to be subsumed in the creativity of her husband. She also began to enjoy her emergence from the shadows of social disgrace. She could more and more show to any relatives and acquaintances who entertained doubts about her marriage that she had backed a winner. This gave her additional authority. But it was the authority of middle age.

When Elgar was at the outset of his great period of creative energy Alice found that she was settled into the prison-house of provincial respectability. She found less time to write, and less to write about. And what she did write carried a continual sense of sadness. Alice's daughter found the restrictions of childhood irksome. Alice herself found the discipline imposed by family responsibility and public accountability irksome too.

After the high spirits of the "Bavarians" Alice wrote a sad little poem, *Sighs in Summer*, which ends

> I haste and ask the swallow,
> And ask the honied bee,
> Marked they sweet eyes grown hollow,
> Eyes tear-stained, did they see?
>
> They neither pause nor hearken,
> Nor birds nor winds can dream
> What cares my heart can darken
> Though summer reign supreme.

Edward saw the poem—no doubt it was put before him as a possibility for a song—but wrote on the margin of the typescript, "If zu smells sis, zu'll find its not fesh! grrh!" In May 1897 she wrote *Love alone*, of which Elgar's setting was published in *The Dome*[4] in January 1898, and subsequently incorporated into *Sea Pictures*.

[4] *The Dome, a Quarterly containing Examples of all the* Arts (Unicorn Press) had published a Minuet by Elgar in 1897.

Malvern
Friday

Dear Troyte:

The Dome has asked me to contribute an extraordinary concoction which simmereth gaily in my brain: but I'm not sure if I *can* do it: we are not going to leave until Monday so come to lunch & would you bring some Indian ink & a pen wherewith you would print some lettering for *fac-simile* for me if my brain works well & acronycally—there's no time to be lost as the MS. (if done at all) must go forth on Sunday.

Yrs. ever
Ed. Elgar

Rosa Burley was associated with this song, to the extent that on 30 May 1897, having brought Carice home from The Mount she sang it with the ink still wet on the manuscript. Some occasional translations from German and Italian appeared spasmodically from Alice in the following years. In 1901 came *Love in Absence*, in which there is a note of anxiety and doubt.

When shall I see the gladdening smile which lies
On thy too pensive brow while joys arise
In hurrying tumult in our souls? Lo! then,
All wondered at the grace Love gives, dear friend,
I kiss away the sadness from thine eyes,
And scarcely caring more for future years
With that one gladness locked within my heart
The world may take its way.

On 16 February 1901, Elgar was at Bradford for a concert of his works—including four of the *Sea Pictures*, sung by Muriel Foster. On that day, alone at home, Alice wrote a poignant "sea picture". The opening of the second stanza recalls one of her earlier poems. Entitled *Reconciliation?* in tentative pencil on the typed copy, the poem runs as follows:

Come back, the sea lies still,
Rests, and forgets its pain,
Winds scarcely fan the hill
The pines may sleep again.
Come back to me, my love at last,
Peace follows storm, forget the angered past.

Come back, and lay thy hand,
As thou wast wont,—just so,

Within mine own; then stand
And smile, and whisper, "Lo,
Forgot, dear heart, is pain and strife,"
Come back, for dreams, give me thyself and life.

The manuscript, as was often the case, was left lying about, with a pencil note in Alice's hand, "Words free!"

One other piece of Alice's calls for comment. This is an essay written somewhere in the mid-nineties, entitled *The Ideal in the Present*. Characteristically—as in the old days of *Marchcroft Manor* with its quiverful of quotations—she sets it in motion with the last three lines in Italian, from Canto XIV in Dante's *Purgatorio*.

Alice's talent was reflective rather than creatively original. Nevertheless, even though her views on matters of philosophy or sociology might not convey anything new in themselves, they do enable us to see her personality as it developed. In *The Ideal in the Present* there is a hardening of attitude, a defiant declaration of faith in élitism—in the "ideal".

> . . . Yet in the midst of our hurried life and massive incomprehension of lofty art, we must remember with joy and astonishment that there is an ideal side even to this age, weary, worn out and sordid as it seems in many respects.
>
> The 'ideal', however, is still manifested in art, and . . . it is one of the glories of the time and a hope of salvation amongst the darker aspects of the age that this is true, though alas! its influence is far from all pervading. To see that we need only go round the rooms of the Academy or those of any other Exhibition. The appalling commoness [*sic*] of subjects will oppress the mind with a weary weight. To what a vast mass of people the pictures with their terrible suburban flavour must appeal. Drawing room and nursery scenes without an intuition of poetic story or artistic teaching prevail, scenes void happily of harm, but replete with common domestic vulgarity.

How much superior, thought Alice, were the contents of the pictures she had seen in the most recent Exhibitions in Munich.[5] However there were at least two noble painters in England:

[5] At the Munich International Art Exhibition Scottish painters (Orchardson, Gregory, Murray, East, Vos, Stott, T. Brown) did well in 1892, but the medals were mostly won by Belgian and Dutch painters.

Burne-Jones and Watts. Rosetti only failed to reach their high standards because his pictures "did not represent so entirely and imaginative side of life and thought. . . ." She returned to an old favourite, *The Golden Stairs* (see p. 65), to rhapsodise on its intimations of spirituality. Thereafter she described with relish *The Days of Creation*, and *Love among the Ruins*. Then it was the turn of Watts. Think, she commands, and throws in a major item in the Elgarian terminology, "of the Enigma, 'the embodied striving of the mind of man to pierce the Unseen, the Unknowable'" in *Hope*. In *Love and Life* she asks us to observe "the ideal of Love in its best and highest influence, saving, leading, and raising its fellow soul through the difficulties and over the stony and steep paths of the world". Edward himself was at times apt to linger on the Wattsian concept of "soul", and one is, perhaps, allowed to wonder whether he and Alice were in agreement on her next dogma.

> To Watts also belongs the rare glory that in the representation of the nude female figure, he clothes it with such a noble ideality that far from its having a debasing influence, or appealing to any lower side of human nature, it stands vested with a sacred purity, an Emblem as it were, of what should be encompassed with reverence.

In respect of modern literature Alice had a prevision of the language of some contemporary moralists. "Never, it will be said," she groaned, "has such a wide stream of unwholesome, loathsome impurities been poured out, glossed over as the work of a new art and with a new prefix to the indispensible 'ism'." But a "good book" will carry all before it. J. H. Shorthouse's *John Inglesant* (pub. 1881) and *Sir Percival* (pub. 1886), were given unconditional merit awards. Mrs. Humphrey Ward's *Robert Elsmere* (1888) (mis-spelt as Ellesmere by Alice) was regarded with more circumspection. With this book, Mrs. Ward, who was a niece of Thomas Arnold, attained notoriety because of its dependence on religious doubts for its tragic conflict. About this Alice was clearly unhappy, but:

> Even a book like this, which promises to teach a new Gospel, however lamentable a failure such an attempt must be from the outset, is more eagerly devoured than the mere passionate tale of lower life, as however mistakenly, its endeavours to supply

the soul with food, for which, unconfessed to itself, Humanity hungers now, as it ever has done.

It will be remembered that Edward was not infrequently disturbed by a sequence of doubts as to the true and the false in religious doctrine.

The last part of her essay is devoted to idealism in music, and, since it can do no other than mirror the thoughts of her husband, it is given in full.

To touch upon the last though one of the greatest forms of Art, we must perceive that Music has entered upon a new phase. Her exponents have attempted to attain spheres hitherto undreamed of & to express feelings, thoughts & passions & to portray histories & tragedies of life in an entirely new method. This new direction, however immensely expanded in our own days, cannot be said to date from our own age but was inaugurated by Beethoven. But instead of a rapid progression in the direction of the Ideal, we may say that nothing so nearly approaching it has been written as his C minor Symphony. The music working through successive phases of beauty to the inspired climax in which all personal longings & passions are forgotten in the vast enthusiasm of reconciled & rejoicing humanity.

In this new world it must be admitted the purely Ideal does not reign supreme. The great Operas are made to reflect with as much realism as possible the stories and feelings on which they are founded—vast fragments of past mythological ages or of medieval romance demand & have obtained the most marvellous representations but they soar into no ideal regions but have us racked & at the last stage of tension & exhausted emotions from sympathy with the agonies & disappointments of the beings who figure in them—their sheer humanity appealing so strongly to us. Parsifal is of course outside the range of these operas as well as of all purely ideal subjects as it presents a great spiritual allegory & treating of religious truth & teaching which are based on other than Ideal inspiration.

In lesser works we have entered upon a phase of programme music often enchanting and delightful but picturing scenes and emotions with which we are all acquainted. The great works of Brahms & also of Max Bruch will readily occur to the mind as exceptions. Brahms attains to a pure intellectuality based on no romance nor calling in the aid of any of the scenes which might be called from the world around us. We are led into a region of pure and abstract thought. Into the same region are we led also by the noble, inspiring strains of Max Bruch to a sphere in which everything ignoble must be lost to sight and the soul can be steeped & strengthened anew for its onward journey.

Elgar's views on Beethoven and Brahms are well known. In 1894 he was made particularly aware of Bruch because of playing music by that composer with George Sinclair. It will be concluded that Elgar could hardly move far from the departments of oratorio and symphony, or the ennobling subsection of 'patriotic' art, without incurring Alice's disapproval. A too close attention to her views on aesthetics ran him into trouble in his lecture on Brahms's Third Symphony at Birmingham on 8 November 1905, when Ernest Newman was present and delighted to expatiate on his own philosophy in the next day's *Manchester Guardian*, pointing out by implication how superior it was to Elgar's.[6] Alice did not much like Newman after that.

[6] See *A Future for English Music*, p. 96f.

10

The Price of Celebrity

During the reign of Edward VII—with whom he was on friendly terms—Elgar came to the zenith of his fame. Outwardly it was an automatic progress by way of oratorios, symphonic works (such as justified the appellation "classical"), a prolific flow of pieces for the music-making proletariat, a Chair founded especially for his accommodation, increasing recognition overseas, influential friends, and honours bestowed by academic bodies as well as by the Monarch. Any normal wife should have been delighted, particularly since her own contribution was not inconsiderable. Alice had the pleasure of being present on most occasions when Edward was fêted. She collected all that was written about him. She performed many of the chores attendant on creative activity. She protected Edward as far as she was able. But—although it only occurred to her on rare occasions—she gradually but effectively destroyed her own personality. She became the romantic biographer's ideal of the "true wife of genius".

Alice kept her sorrows to herself. Edward's moods needed to be understood—and mostly they were (but not always by Alice). The fact that balancing the household budget required particular application and skill was disguised from the world. From time to time Alice fell ill—and the cause inevitably was "worry". She "worried herself to death" whenever Edward was away from home, and this feeling was conveyed to Carice who knew

> by painful experience . . . what it was like when he was away. One could hardly get an answer about anything and until his telegram came saying he was safely in London—or wherever it was—she was terribly on edge, and seemed to think that one was very unfeeling if one did not appear to be worried about the journey. If she ever allowed herself to throw off this terrible worrying, she could be the most delightful companion, but unfortunately this did not very often happen.

Elgar found his own means of escape from the pressures of creativity and domesticity. In the early years of the century he spent many summer hours bicycling round the countryside, and *The Apostles* has some claim to be regarded as the only major oratorio generated from this exercise. Sometimes he rode with the Malvern, the Speedwell, or the Swifts Cycling Clubs, and sometimes his companion was Troyte Griffith, with whom he shared a great interest in medieval architecture. Troyte Griffith wrote:

> Elgar told me that he really composed the Apostles sitting in the porch of Queen Hill Church near Longdon. He used to ride there on his bicycle.

Concerning this work Griffith also remembered how:

> While he was writing the Apostles, a new church was being built near Craeg Lea (at Lower Wyche). I said to Elgar that I would ask the Vicar to have it dedicated to the Apostles. Elgar said 'Well if he agrees, I will deposit the MSS. full score in the church, but you mustn't tell him I have said so'. All Saints was chosen as the dedication. When I told Elgar he said 'That's just like the C. of E. You've got no saints of your own, so you grab the whole lot at one fell swoop'.

Of another bicycling excursion Griffith left another anecdote, suggesting that the disciplinary standards in some of the exclusive girls' schools of Malvern were not as high as parents expected them to be, and proprietors of such schools claimed that they were.

> We bicycled from Hereford to see a 14th century building attached to a farm house. When we came out the daughter of the house asked us to come in for tea. Rather to my surprise Elgar accepted the invitation. After tea he offered a cigarette to our hostess with the words 'I know you smoke'. When we got outside I said to him 'You have never seen that girl before why did you say you knew she smoked?' That's all you know about it.' said Elgar 'She was at Miss ——' school at Malvern and all the girls there smoked'.

Elgar went bicycling with the Hoopers and with Miss Wilson who were the Elgars' neighbours, and also with Rosa Burley. Miss Burley held a somewhat privileged position in the household since she was firmly in control of Carice's development. A constant visitor both at "Forli" and "Craeg Lea", with a growing belief in the ultimate value of Elgar's music, and disbelief in Alice's capacity to understand either her husband or his music, Rosa Burley built herself into the romantic role of the great composer's confidante. Dora Penny ("Dorabella") put up a spirited claim to primacy in this function, but she was resident in Wolverhampton for the most part. Rosa Burley frequently

Pattern for a Bag-Poet.

accompanied the Elgars on holiday, and in the years that saw the creation of *The Apostles* and *The Kingdom*, the *Introduction and Allegro* and *In the South*, she was very much on hand. (A curious undated allusion to the "Welsh tune" of the string work, found among Alice's papers, is shown on the previous page.) When, on 24 June 1902, news of the necessary postponement of the *Coronation Ode* broke, Rosa was with Elgar. She wrote:

> The Ode was written and was to be performed at a grand concert at Covent Garden I think. Edward was to conduct the Ode and wear Court dress. This pleased him very much.
>
> We went for a bicycle ride and had tea at an Inn. People were already going up to London in great numbers.
>
> E. was in a good mood and looking forward to the next day. While we were having tea I suddenly said to him, "Don't be disappointed if there is some hitch about tomorrow. I can't believe that the King can go through such a programme. Think! He goes down to Spithead & reviews the Fleet in the morning. Salutes being fired all the time. Sunshine blazing on the sea. Then in the afternoon he comes up by train to London. Then dinner, eight courses remember. Then he goes to Covent Garden and has a long affair [*sic*] to listen to and presentations to be made. I can't see him doing it all."
>
> We had just finished tea and were preparing to go when the landlady rushed in saying "Oh! Sir. The Coronation is put off, the King is ill and is to have an operation at once. The news is just in at the Post Office." This was consternation indeed, Edward was very calm and said, "Well; I shall have a few days bicycling that's all".

In the book that was made from Miss Burley's memories Edward was made to appear anything but calm. However, it was agreed both by Miss Burley and by Alice—in her diary—that in the next few days a good many miles were ridden by Edward and Rosa. Occasionally one is able to catch glimpses of the life of the community on a realistic plane. Alice's eye for detail was not what it had been in her novel-writing days, but Carice had inherited her powers of observation. On 6 September 1903, while staying at Hereford for the Three Choirs Festival, Alice, Edward and Carice, were walking back to 44 Bridge Street (a house lent by the Misses Underwood and Thomas) from Mass at Belmont; by the wayside, Carice related how they saw a woman sitting in the ditch making tea and eating raw turnips. "Father had a long talk to her."

During the Birmingham Festival—at which *The Apostles* was given its first performance—Alice went into the Cathedral and noted how the Burne-Jones window with the representation of the Ascension "seemed to illustrate E's music".[1] But Edward emerged from the Festival tired and dispirited about his finances. He was further depressed at the news of the death of his Liverpool friend Rodewald. As it had been in the case of Alice and her mother twenty years before, the cure for depression was a holiday in Italy. At the end of November, Alice and Edward travelled to Bordighera—already familiar to Alice—by way of Paris and Marseilles. Here they stayed for some days looking for a furnished villa, but after seeing only those that were either unclean or unapproachable, except by mule track, they settled on the Villa Giovanni in Alassio. The agents installed a cook (Alice herself was totally incapable in the kitchen), the Elgars wrapped themselves up in fur coats at night time (because the stoves were out of action), looked out of the windows at familiar pouring rain, and prepared to enjoy themselves. Edward orchestrated *Fly Singing Bird* and *The Snow*, thus recalling to Alice her own days of youthful aspiration, and just before Christmas Miss Burley arrived, bringing Carice with her.

The holiday turned out better than had at one time seemed likely, as is indicated in a letter from Alice to Martina Hyde, the co-founder, with Winifred Norbury, of the Worcestershire Philharmonic Society.

Alassio Jan 17: 1904

My dear Miss Hyde

I am so glad to hear such good news of the W[orcestershire] P[hilharmonic] S[ociety] & am writing to say may my Subn. wait till we return, when I will not, all being well, forget it. It is really a trial getting P.O. here, the P. Office is a *most* remarkable institution & always closes from 12 to 3, & sometimes till 4 or 5! We have had some very nice weather & some most *lovely* walks & excursions. We have enjoyed them immensely. The views are so splendid & we can sit & bask & rest in the sun & disbelieve in winter. It is a little cold again

[1] The "Ascension" window, one of four by Burne-Jones in this church, was installed in the chancel of Birmingham Cathedral in 1884.

today but I hope it will not last. The air is very invigorating & delightful & I am glad to say Edward & Carice do full justice to its goodness & hope they will go on doing so.

Please remember me to Mrs. Hyde & yr. sisters & self.

Yrs. very sincly.

C. Alice Elgar.

Having returned to Malvern—that the maid was ill was a relatively major disaster—Alice almost immediately began to show signs of restlessness. She was in a house-hunting frame of mind, and chose Hanley Swan for her first forays. But Edward did not like a house that was on offer there. Alice turned her attention next to Hereford, where she consulted Miss Underwood, and while Edward was writing out the score of *In the South*, the attractions of one house in particular—Plas Gwyn—were becoming increasingly alluring. Edward concentrated on his rapidly spiralling progress towards eminence, by way of royal approval and aristocratic interest, dinner parties with the great, and Richter's promotion of Elgarian claims at the Covent Garden Elgar Festival. Alice took Troyte and other friends to inspect the house at Hereford, and to arrange with Gurney the landlord the details of necessary improvements and of the lease.

Elgar was given an honorary doctorate at Durham that year, made a member of the Athenaeum, and in midsummer he was knighted. During the spring—in spite of his public success—Edward was edgy and irritable. The weather was not good. A few days in the West Country—at Bath and Weston-super-Mare—merely increased his irritability. A trip to Longdon Marsh left him more miserable, for the countryside was now disfigured by telegraph poles and wires, and the clock face on the church tower had been repainted. When in May Steinbach (with whom Elgar became a Vice-President of the Mainz Handel Society that year) performed *Gerontius* in Cologne in the composer's presence, Elgar, displeased with the performance, refused to show up on the rostrum in acknowledgement of the enthusiasm of the audience.

Before leaving Malvern, Alice sent a selection of her poems to some unidentifiable publisher. The proposed anthology, however, never materialised. All that survives to indicate the intention is the list which accompanied the poems.

POEMS sent by Mrs. Edward Elgar,
Craeg Lea,
Wells Road
Malvern.

The Mill Wheel, Winter
" " May
The Dying Warriors (translation)
Atalanta's Race
"Thy love doth fade"
On the Way
Sonnet translated from Dante
The Sunny Isles
1588
To emulate Marcus Aurelius
The Fight for the Shrine
A Courtyard in Granada
Love and Death
Love's Grace
Sighs in Summer
Ways to the Mount (Sonnet)
"The friend of the bridegroom"—(Sonnet)
Renunciation
"Something afar."

The task which took much time and combined thought was the selection of furniture for Plas Gwyn, which was ready for occupation in July. Carice wrote how:

> The new house was in a residential area of Hereford on a road that only led to small villages and was consequently quiet. It was a three storey house with a basement and would make into flats very easily as each floor was exactly alike. The two downstairs sitting-rooms, Mother's drawing-room, and Father's study had a balcony running right round with creepers. It was a nice garden lawn in front and a sizeable kitchen garden and stables useful for storage. . . . As usual, Mother had to start on a round of calls, everyone seemed to come and call. . . .

Plas Gwyn gave out onto the river where there was a ferry to take one to Rotherwas or to Billingham. Alice loved the house (despite its expense in upkeep), and the garden where the greenfinches built their nests. In order to keep the household running smoothly Alice had Edward's niece May Grafton to live in. It was intended that she should supervise some part of Carice's instruction who was expected soon to leave Miss Burley's establishment. (In the latter part of 1905 May and Alice were kept at full stretch in making copies of Edward's lectures for Birmingham University[2]). Further to strengthen Carice for the rigours of life her mother decided that on Saturday mornings she should attend the gymnasium of the Hereford High School for gymnastics. It is clear that life in a cathedral city in some aspects—as Mrs. Henry Wood suggested—left a good deal to be desired.

> It was absolute torture to me in those days, for I had no idea of marching in time and the idea of a running jump at the horse so paralysed me with fright that I just could not do it. I used to dread Saturday mornings to which my poor cousin May always had to take me because I was not allowed to go into Hereford alone down St. Owen's Street because in those days there were so many drunk people about even at eight or nine in the morning.

While Alice was thus disposing of her daughter she was ensuring that Edward's likeness was preserved for posterity. Family portraiture was part of the tradition to which she had been accustomed (the subject was dealt with in her own *The Portrait*) and it was fitting that a painting of Sir Edward should complement that of Sir Henry Gee Roberts. Talbot Hughes, a veteran of the Grosvenor Gallery Exhibitions, and expert in musical subjects (e.g. *The Symphony*, of 1888), came to Plas Gwyn and worked in the drawing-room which Alice transformed into a temporary studio.

It was a triumphant year for Edward, with a visit to the United States and a Mediterranean cruise as a guest of the Royal Navy, but he remained obstinately depressed. After an American tour that was undertaken unwillingly Alice was in despair. She called in the doctor who prescribed a rest cure in Radnorshire, and after inspection by Alice and May Grafton a house was duly rented in New Radnor. But the high hopes entertained of this respite in the country were frustrated by Edward's slipping on wet stones, and injuring his knee. So back they went to Hereford.

During that time Carice was removed from Malvern and put into Hereford High School for Girls, where, under a Miss

[2] See *A Future for English Music*, ed. Percy M. Young, London 1968.

Krabbe's watchful eye, she would be able to supplement her gymnastics with academic subjects. Conscious of her responsibility to distinguished parents Miss Krabbe used often to cut short her lunch hours to try to improve Carice's arithmetic.

The reason for Carice's change of school was the collapse of The Mount. Back from New Radnor, Edward discovered that Miss Burley had disappeared not only from Malvern, but also from England.

June 1906 | Plas Gwyn
Hereford

Dear Miss Burley,

We only arrived home last Monday night & are overwhelmed with accumulations of letters. We were so sorry to hear you had departed and are quite at sea as to your movements: we would like to know more. Miss Homer wrote to Carice and I have your note about the chair which can be case-housed until you claim it. I don't understand what you mean by having "bought" it: did you have a sale? I have seen no one from Malvern—Mr. Griffith is, I suppose, away as I have sent him a p.c. and had no reply.

I do trust you are settling down happily in Portugal & shall be glad to know your affairs here are more peacefully settled than you anticipated, as to the cheque please do not think of that.

The American visit was quite successful but since then I have been very ill—now better.

I am working away but I do not feel settled down to it yet.

I am having the [*lacuna*] sent out to you & shall not expect it again as we will see it first.

With all good wishes
Believe me
Yours very sincerely
Edward Elgar.

July was full of visitors, who included Mrs. Worthington and Professor Sanford from the United States, Frank Schuster (one of Edward's wealthy friends, a homosexual dilettante whom Alice did not like), and the Stuarts of Wortley. All of them heard parts of the almost completed *The Kingdom*, and all were greatly impressed. On 17 July Elgar wrote again to Rosa Burley.

Dear Miss Burley,

I am glad to receive your enquiries, & so glad to say I am better: it was a silly accident, simply going out of the door & I fell, smash!

It had been raining & the smooth stones were very wet. It was in Radnor where we had a cottage for a fortnight. I was brought here & had horrid massage from a Nurse Parkin twice a day. Now I can get about again but have not cycled yet. *I have no one to cycle with.*

The world seems very old to me now and all (so) changed. I had a horrid chill coming from America and have been very very ill. It seems so curious I don't *smoke* now! Can you believe it! I cannot, but I have no wish for it.

All you say about Faro [town on the southern coast of Portugal] is most interesting to me: Tell me if you think of staying any time or if it is only a temporary visit.

Everybody is out and it is a hot sunny afternoon and reminds me of some summer days in The [Longdon] Marsh, & at Birchwood, so long, long ago.

My work nears completion & will send it to you as soon as it is ready; is there any duty to pay or anything? I was afraid to send any trifles for fear you would have to pay more than their absurd value. I suppose you don't wear gloves! only mantilla and fans.

We have had our American friends here & shewed them some of our County but I fear I make a poor guide now. I seem *tired*—oh! so tired [.] everything is so useless. I was away when your trying time at Malvern came & it is a grief to me to know that I was unable to do anything.

Carice is very busy with her studies & swimming & all sorts of things & she is very strong & full of vitality & revels in any amount of work. Everything goes on as usual. I think Mr. Griffith *may* leave Malvern as his partner Mr. [lacuna] is giving up the agency there. I saw Winifred [Norbury] and Mr. Hyde at the Festival practice here and all seems to [lacuna] on. I hope you are happy in your surroundings—I gather so. You know I wish you everything good now & always.

[copy ends here]

Two more letters to Rosa Burley followed during that year. The first written on 19 August was as follows:

Dear Miss Burley,
I have asked the publishers to send you some music—if it is not what you require throw it away and let me know.

I am quite well again having [lacuna] money from the "acculented" [*sic*]. I will very gladly send Miss Homer a ticket but I hope she will remind me of it nearer the time. I have *so* much to do proof-reading etc. I send a copy of the Birmingham Programme book.

If you remember the Alassio fishermen you will also recollect that Mr. Congreve told us that they went to Spain or somewhere tunny-fishing during some part of the year: so you may meet the Alassio friends.

We are altogether and they send messages

Yours very sincerely,
Edward Elgar

In September Elgar went to Manchester for orchestral rehearsals for *The Kingdom*, of which the first performance was to take place at the Birmingham Festival on 25 September. "The players," wrote Alice in her Diary, "broke into uncontrollable applause now and again".

Edward returned to the Midland Hotel and wrote rather less ecstatically:

Dear Miss Burley:

The rehearsal is over—that is to say the orchestral one & the new thing sounds well. I have been awfully busy and could not write a p.c. to say I sent you some papers and hope they come safely. Do not trouble to thank me for them.

We have not heard of you for a long time but hope that you are well.

Miss Homer came to the Hereford Festival and I was delighted to see her: but I was torn in many pieces by numbers of people who [lacuna] to abound at such times but I missed you and thought of Gloucester (after your Hungarian rhapsody) and Worcester last year when we gave you a motor-ride. Send a p.c. & [lacuna] to remember I shall think of you on Wednesday morning in Birmingham when the new work is heard.

Kindest regards
Yours sincerely [?]
Ed. Elgar

P.S. I am travelling through the night to Aberdovey.

At the time, for reasons of health, the Elgars were staying in Wales.

At the end of the year hopes of an Italian holiday waxed and waned; but as Christmas approached chances seemed remote, as Edward wrote to Noble, the organist of York Minster:

Hereford
Dec 22
1906

My dear Noble:

I was delighted to receive your letter & hope you are better & the chill gone.

I have been having troublesome gout in the eyelids

& must not use my eyes for any fine work, reading or writing; so I am practically resting.

All your musical news interests me very much & I am really glad you like my music—some peoples opinions I do *not* value, but yours I do extremely.

The Italian tour cannot come off but I may go to India on Dec: 31 I will let you hear.

My wife joins me in kindest regards to Mrs. Noble yourself & the small one who must be growing up!

Yours ever
Edward Elgar

When the New Year came, however, Italy was again on. After spending most of January and February there, Elgar went once more to the United States, and then followed the normal home festival circuit.

It was the year in which the matter of the Birmingham Chair hung over the family like a thunder cloud; but the year in which the First Symphony was being formulated. There were lesser works too; like the part-songs of Op. 53 and Op. 54, as well as *How calmly the evening*, and *Love*—a setting of words by Arthur Macquarie—and some Anglican chants. *Love* was incorporated into the body of Elgar's works as Op. 18, No. 2, thus becoming companion to *O Happy Eyes* of long ago. The significance of the coupling of the new piece with the old is enhanced by the dedication—to C. A. E. She, for her part, was almost pathetically grateful for the acknowledgement, feeling "very unworthy & deeply touched". A few days later the fourth of the Pomp and Circumstance Marches was completed, this being inscribed to Sinclair, the Hereford organist.

On 2 August Rosa Burley heard again from Elgar:

Dear Miss Burley

Since I last wrote—which must be in the dark ages—we have heard with much interest of your travels. I should like to see Portugal very much & Lisbon especially. I knew the town so well since I could speak and before that, as we had a friend who was tutor or something at some College there in the sixties!

I came back from America safely & without adventures . . . we have been trying to endure the summer but it has been hard and trying to work, so cold & wet. Carice rides a bicycle very well and joins me in my lonely expedition. . . .

I am sorry Mr. [Jaeger] is so ill and although a little improvement is reported I fear he is in an unsatisfactory condition although the new place suits him better than Davos. I suppose it is getting late for your talked of English visit. You have not missed much at it has happened. I never remember such a dreary time, & you must return in sunshine and flowers. We talk of a little fortnight's change but we do not make it; but it is something to think about.

I am doing little work now: my eyes are not workable and I do not improve.

Kindest regards
Yours sincerely
Edward Elgar

As a matter of fact, Carice was rather less expert than her father suggests, for on 13 July, when the two of them were on a long excursion she "collided with an old man on a tricycle". No one, luckily, was hurt.

The "little fortnight's change", more or less, was arranged, in Wales, before the Gloucester Festival. From Gloucester, bearing proofs of the first *Wand of Youth* suite and sketches of the symphony, to London; from London to Cardiff; and then, from Plas Gwyn; on 27 September:

My dear Miss Burley

Very many thanks for the "roes" which are famous: I am just passing through Hereford on my way to London. It seemed strange being on Welsh land (!) again & I remembered the last time I saw Cardigan from further south.[3]

I wish the weather would be a little more [lacuna] to you from the south: it *has* been a most dreary year. We had hoped we should have seen you.

I find rehearsals for [Leeds?] are on the 3rd, 4th, & 5th. I return on the morning (10 a.m.) of the 5th to St. Andrew's Hall.

Again thanks & kindest regards,
Sincerely yours
Edward Elgar

At the beginning of November the Elgars went to Rome, where, after protest from Alice concerning the difficulties of obtaining efficient domestic help, they stayed until the middle of May. Once settled in the Via Gregoriana they suffered a spasm of nostalgia, and remembering obligations to Sinclair

[3] Reference to the holiday spent at Llangranog, with Rosa Burley and her relatives, in 1901: see *Letters to Nimrod*, pp. 140–2.

and his choristers jointly produced A *Christmas Greeting*. Completed on 8 December it did not leave much time for rehearsal in Hereford for the Carol Concert for which it was intended. However, the significance of this piece is the re-emergence of Alice as a poet. The process of evolution was the same as in the case of the "Bavarians".

The first extant sketch runs thus:

[Emb] Bowered on [the] sleeping hillside rise
In sunny glow, the purpling vine:
[In] [Under your] Beneath the greyer [skies] English skies
In fair array the red gold apples shine.

On & on [the] [The] old Tiber flows
[Troubled] Dark with [ancient haunting] its weight of
ancient crime
Far north, through green and quiet meads
Speeds on the Wye midst mists & silvering rime.

Continued in pencil

The Pfifferari come from far
They seek the shrines & [piping] hymn the peace
Which Herald Angels 'neath the Star
[Proclaim [ed] ing [ed] to men [and sang] in song that
strife should cease]
Foretold to shepherds bidding strife [should] to cease
[The northern land is] [O'er] [The quiet landscape] steal]
sleeps in white]
[The sounds] The bells from
Sweet village bells sound o'er the snow
And Noel Noel echoes through the night

Next comes a fair copy by Alice, with annotation (shown here in italics) by Edward:

I Bowered on sloping hillsides rise
In sunny glow, the purpling vine;
II Beneath the greyer English skies,
In fair array, the red-gold apples shine.
refrain
I On and on old Tiber [flows] *speeds,*
Dark with its[4] weight of ancient crime:

[4] In published setting—the

II Far north, through green and quiet meads,
Speeds Flows on the Wye midst mists and silvering rime.
refrain
II The[P[f]ifferari] *pifferari* come from[5] far,
They seek the shrines and hymn the peace
Which [H]herald [A]angels, 'neath the [S]star
Foretold to shepherds, bidding strife to cease.
II Our England sleeps in shroud of snow,
Bells, sadly sweet, recall life's flight[6]
And tears, unbid, are wont to flow
As 'Noel, Noel' sounds across the night.
refrain

Rome
6 Dec.
1907

I and *II* respectively indicate that first or second voice commences the phrase. On a separate sheet is the refrain, written in pencil:

To you in snow
To us in sun
Love is but one.
[The year dies slow]
Hearts beat & glow
By oak or vine
[As comes the]
Friends for always mine.[7]

Throughout 1908 Alice fretted about Edward's recurring depressions. Now resigned to going to church alone—or with Carice—she felt a sense of separateness. She dutifully went with Edward to most places for professional or social reasons and watched and wondered at the growth and the appearance of the First Symphony. This was a "noble and beautiful" work—the very summation of all she had defined in her essay of ten years or so previously. Betweenwhiles Alice read aloud so as to relieve

[5] —wander.
[6] Knell life's swift flight.
[7] To—Those in snow,
To those in sun,
Love is but one;
Hearts beat and glow,
By oak or palm,
Friends in storm or calm.

the too sober air of concentration, choosing Somerville and Ross—*Reminiscences of an Irish J.P.*, as she called it. Somewhat more relief came in August with the shedding of the Birmingham Professorship.

The next year continued to be trying on the domestic front. At the beginning of March, just after Edward had spent a couple of days in bed, the cook, Mrs. Sandals, startled everyone by coming home drunk, and when reprimanded by Edward, shrieking abuse at, and threatening with a chair, her employers. The police were informed and the last that was seen of Mrs. Sandals was in a cab and under arrest. Not long after this there was opportunity to go again to Italy, this time as the guest of Mrs. Worthington—a wealthy American friend—who had a villa at Careggi. Familiarly Julia Worthington was "Pippa".

> Careggi proved an ideal place, a long drive out of Florence opposite Fiesole. . . . It was wonderful summer weather, & the nightingales sang all night & if they ever paused, the frogs filled in the gap. Pippa arranged for a carozza to be at our disposal every day, so some one of the party could always go into Florence for shopping or sightseeing. My father was thoroughly happy here & wrote music which always seems to me to be in a particular vein of its own, viz, *Go Song of Mine* (Op. 57), and *Angelus* (Op. 56). He spent much time at the piano, improvising & playing his favourite music. I shall never [forget] his playing of the Coriolan Overture, he had a gift of making the piano sound as though the whole orchestra was there. He & my Mother made a detour to Pisa & Bologna; I stayed with Pippa & we all met again in Venice, with which he was disappointed because you could not see the beauty for the people; with the result that we were up at five one morning so as to walk round without interference. . . . We made our way slowly home via Verona & renewing their acquaintance with the Bavarian Highlands, which they found rather spoilt with a lot of building, since they were there in the early nineties. We paid a solemn call on Richard Strauss and his wife, my mother being their interpreter. We were amused when Strauss wanted to show my Father some score or paper of interest, he called out to Frau Strauss who produced a bunch of keys from her underskirt, & duly locked it all up again when they had finished. Back in London, they engaged a young Frenchman Arsène Jaulnay, to be valet who proved a great success & we settled down to life at Hereford again. I unfortunately contracted scarlet fever just before the Hereford Festival, & instead of the nice party at Plas Gwyn for which all sorts of preparations had been made, my Mother took a

large house near the Cathedral and my Father went there with the party, leaving my poor Mother in quarantine with me. I was only allowed to talk to the various friends over the gate, to say nothing of missing all the music & festivities. This quarantine seems to have lasted until 4 October when my Mother was at last released. She was able to go to Birmingham for the festival & was so relieved at being free to go out again that she said she even enjoyed the train journey.[8]

During that year, inspired by London's new Kingsway—which had been opened by the King some four years earlier—Alice (using a nom de plume, "Charles Alison", for this poem) wrote *The Kingsway* (altered to *The King's Way*). This stirring chauvinistic ballad—a proper piece for a Major-General's daughter—attracted both Arthur Boosey—who could not have it set to music by Edward and published soon enough—and Edward. The manuscript carries an appendage by Edward:

Mem
England's sons across the sea;
They too will fight and keep it free:
Let every voice in England say,—
"God keep the way, by night and day,
The King of England's Way!"
The King's Way.

In that year there was a distinct worsening of the international atmosphere, and the thought of war with Germany occurred to some as a real possibility. It was otherwise a sad year since a number of old and valued friends died. They were Jaeger, Basil Nevinson, and Alice's uncle and aunt Robert and Henriette Raikes. Robert Raikes had been a General in the Bengal Army in which Henriette's father had been a Major.

By 1910 the life style of the Elgar family was necessarily adapted to the requirements of an eminence that was to be further distinguished in the next year by the award of the Order of Merit. Edward had to spend more and more time in London, so arrangements were made for periods of residence in New Cavendish Street, in Queen Anne's Mansions, or Gloucestershire. While Edward and Alice were in London (or being entertained in the country by the wealthy) Carice was often deposited on relatives or friends. After the completion of the Violin Concerto

[8] Carice Elgar Blake's MS. Notes.

in the summer of 1910 while her parents went to stay with Lady Mary Trefusis (formerly Lygon) in Cornwall, Carice went down to the Forest of Dean and crotchety old Aunt Caroline Dighton. Poor old soul, her dictatorial tendencies had lost for her the companionship of one daughter, and the other was dying of tuberculosis. Aunt Caroline had one son and his wife living with her, but the other son, Richard, was an officer in the army, and very much a man about town. Occasionally he visited the Elgars in London, which pleased Alice, who never tired of having news of those who for her represented the "old days". On another occasion Carice was despatched to Wolverhampton, to the Pennys, oecumenically to assist in the administration of garden fêtes held for the benefit of St. Peter's Church, and to keep Dora Penny up with the news of Edward's projects. In former times Dora had been accustomed on occasion to bicycle to Malvern in order to assist in the rites of composition, and to help entertain the Elgars in Wolverhampton. When the composer achieved fame—because of the various attendant pressures—he was not, she discovered, so accessible as formerly.

There was a growing sense of nostalgia. In London both Alice and Edward longed for their own country, and they paid sentimental visits—to Claines, where Edward as a boy had read scores in the churchyard, and where Whinfield still lived, and to Hasfield. In the summer of 1910 Plas Gwyn was again let, this time to J. S. Arkwright, the Conservative candidate in the General Election.

In Germany in December there was a flash-back. Dr. Charles Grindrod, keeper of a hydropathic establishment at Wyche-side, in Malvern, an enthusiast for natural history and photography was the son of one of those who accompanied W. S. Symonds on his expeditions. He is even mentioned in *Records of the Rocks.* Here, nearly forty years on, his wife reappears on the scene.

Krefeld Dear Troyte:
Dec 16 Good. Next Thursday G. Malvern station
1910 please get the negatives from Mrs. Grindrod for one guinea I don't think we want any other photos.

I am working here with a *huge* German orchestra—as

usual a lot of fierce ones in uniform—but very nice to work with. The symphony goes well.

We return on Sunday night to London.

Hope you will like Salome

Love from Alice &
Edward Elgar

Alice wants to know if Mrs. Grindrod has any large photos framed or otherwise of me? If so will you let us know,

At this time Alice became certain that a house in or near London was essential, and so she dragged round the home counties and the suburbs—High Wycombe, Beaconsfield, Farnham, Weybridge, and Hampstead. From the first round of inspection no properties survived to provide a short list. Alice now brought reinforcements to the task of selection in the person of her old maid Sarah—a relic of Redmarley—and together they tried recommended houses in Kingston, Golders Green, and Oxted. Finally Alice did find what she wanted: a house, named Kelston, in Netherall Gardens, Hampstead, built by Norman Shaw for Edwin Long, the once fashionable painter.

To like the house, and to buy it were two different things, and Alice fought a long legal battle in order to break the terms of a trust. Having won the battle and laid hands on the money she prepared for entry into "E's own house", at the beginning of 1912. She wrote the hope that it might "be happy and beautiful for him". The house was thus described by Carice:

> It was by no means everybody's house as it would only accommodate a small family such as ours as everything was sacrificed to the long stately corridor and the large music room and annexe, a large dining room and large basement, two large bedrooms and three quite small ones, and two even smaller for the staff. The music room was panelled and Mr. Edward Speyer gave my Father a wonderful present by having the small room off the music room fitted with shelves and cupboards to make him a lovely study and library. Every fitting was of finest workmanship, on the floor of the small entrance hall was a wonderful mosaic and on the door itself a marvellous beaten brass design. . . .
>
> I must add there was a small opening off the long corridor where callers were asked to wait if they had come on business. I shall remember it as the place where the nuns, who came every so often to ask for funds, were comfortably settled and given cocoa at my Mother's instructions, however busy we were. They

always seemed to come on days of domestic crisis but nothing interfered with their cocoa.

Alice was not at all pleased that Edward, determined to have the house as he wanted it, sold his old violin, and bought a billiard table. However, friends rallied round in a princely manner, to make the task of appointing the residence less expensive. In addition to Speyer's offering, and numerous smaller gifts, Schuster furnished the drawing room with Empire furniture, and Muriel Foster and her husband provided a settee. Kelston was renamed Severn House, and everyone said what a splendid place it was, and hoped it would prove so to be.

It was, unfortunately, a house with an uneasy reputation. Long had spent much money on it. But when his reputation and his income diminished he and his wife found that they had to live only in one room, and even that imposed a strain on their resources. That was a lesson to creative artists not to try to live above their station.

11

End of the Day

There is a note in Troyte Griffith's papers stating how he made drawings from which a Malvern craftsman named Jacob (may he have his little share of immortality) made an Aeolian harp, a present for Severn House. Elgar drew the theme of the "Enigma" in medieval notation and this was inlaid on the harp. The first Aeolian harp in this story was that which delighted Alice at Hazeldine.

The most significant characteristic of the romantic temperament is the tendency to look back. Towards this tendency both Edward and Alice were partial, and the further they moved through life the more they wondered that changes had been so frequent and so disobliging. Alice's view was within a frame constructed from the remembered rigours of regimental discipline, of country-house propriety, and of a divinely ordained social structure. But somewhere inside the frame was also a blurred image of a girl who had once tripped across the meadows of Gloucestershire full of hope, ideas, and poetry. Somewhere along the way the poet stumbled and never picked herself up again.

Edward was conspicuous in his exemplification of the principle of the divine discontent attributed to the true artist. His successes, he knew, were in spite of himself, and in spite of the world. And insofar as he was successful it was—to the world at large—for the wrong reasons. Edward was honest. He knew the rare quality of his music, but the character of its uniqueness was not for anyone else fully to understand. Certainly not Alice. But Alice continued to believe that she was the true repository of the meaning of Edward's music, which, alas, she could only finally interpret in terms of extreme banality.

The backward glance was responsible for the orchestration

of *The Wind at Dawn* in 1912. In so renewing the impulse of this trifle Edward was reminding himself, and Alice, that he was not indifferent either to her buried ambitions or to the duty he owed her for her loyalty and dedication.

The Music Makers, another recollection of past times, and of old friends, was performed for the first time at the Birmingham Festival that autumn. So on after that event Edward resumed his correspondence with Rosa Burley from the Lake District where the Elgars went from Birmingham to recuperate.

Oct. 13 '12 — Prince of Wales Lake Hotel, Grasmere

My dear Rosa:

We came here after Birmingham for a rest--the first I have had this year [not strictly true]—really & truly I need it very much. Carice is here & received your card which gives me the address. We had the usual Hereford rehearsals and festival which is more pleasant in memories than reality than that of the larger towns. When do you come to England? Shall I ever see you again?

I have this year been very unwell—gout of sorts—& much depressed—I suppose I am old! However I have plenty of vitality if there was any [thing] to feel vital for.

We have had a lovely week of weather but it seems to be getting winterly now & must fly back to London now.

Your travels must have been very interesting & the sound of the names makes me envious, but you will tell me all about it when you come. In the meantime you *might* write! If you don't mind being burdened with useless music I'd send you the new thing *The Music Makers*—You will like the words but you will probably know them already.

E. E.

By the end of the month Miss Burley was back in England and had visited the Elgars at Severn House, after which she retreated to Lincolnshire where, among other activities, she conducted a village choir.

At the beginning of 1913 the Elgars went to Italy in the hope that Edward would be released from the state of depression in which he was currently sunk. No better after his return, he nonetheless undertook the obligations of social life and worked on *Falstaff*, but

Father was still not well and all sorts of remedies were proposed. Eventually he decided to go to Llandridnod Wells and take the waters. He always had a fancy to do this; he went off alone in March and seemed to enjoy the routine of the cure and was always up early for the first drink of the day. It is really impossible to say that there was anything definite wrong with him; it stemmed from digestive troubles which in their turn sprang from the fact that things were not going well; if something favourable happened digestion was forgotten. In the same way, he would complain of a terrible headache but if one could find something to interest him or if something exciting happened, the headache would be quickly forgotten.[1]

In July Edward, absorbed in *Falstaff*, though back on both his hero's and his own adventures of long ago in Gloucestershire.

July 21 '13

Severn House
Hampstead N.W.

My dear Rosa:

Many thanks for your letter which I must acknowledge at once. *I knew*; & the old place holds [lacuna], but you are coming back surely & during the holidays you would be more free than just now. I remember your return from Bruges in the same train which runs, I think—although the service may have been quickened on its arrival might be the same which still exists in London if not in Malvern.

E. E.

Another letter of July returns to the old familiar place—where *The Apostles*, in particular, was mostly sketched.

My dear Rosa:

Yes I remember only the sweetness of it—the spring, then the beans and the hives, I suppose I shall never see it all again or cycle over the old place.

How lovely the [Longdon] Marsh must be—I envy you your seeing it and living in it again. During these two moments I have put in—all the people seem to disappear & only the eternal hills and all the memories of the old loveliness, remains

Yours ever
Ed Elgar

Two months later Elgar acknowledged Miss Burley's reaction to the article on *Falstaff* which had been published that month in *The Musical Times*

[1] Carice Elgar Blake MS.

Sept. 21, 1913 The Hut
Bray
Berks[2]

My dear Miss Burley:

I was so glad to hear you liked the article. There *is* some subtle music floating around. I am sorry you will not be in London for the rehearsal; after Leeds we have no plans, but we shall meet at Leeds & perhaps something definite could be settled.

Please send me anything you write—I have not been home yet to release your MS. but next week when I have got over my rehearsals I shall be able to attend to things. I feel very guilty in having kept it so long. Please find us at Leeds: we shall be at the Metropole Hotel.

If you should change your mind, and why should you not, & come to London next week, let me know. I go home tomorrow.

Always sincerely yours,
Edward Elgar

In October Miss Burley came to stay at Severn House for a couple of nights, after which she went back to her village choir, for which Elgar became unofficial adviser.

Dec. 6 1913 Severn House
Hampstead N.W.

My dear Miss Burley:

I have never sent you a word of thanks for the lovely ducks: they arrived when I was away but I returned in time to eat them —part of them of course. I hope you are well & that the competition preparations progress. I heard from Novello a few days ago that they were now prepared to send *me* all the *music you* are doing. I prevented the flood of melody by rushing to the telephone which for once justified its existence—which is more than I can do. When are you coming to London again?

Best regards
Yours sincerely
Edward Elgar.

A few months later Edward again gave consideration to Miss Burley's village music, and to his own depressed condition.

Feb. 16 '1914 Severn House,
42 Netherall Gardens
Hampstead N.W.

Dear Miss Burley:

I was very glad to receive your letter—but you had much better have brought it, or better still said it. The spring *is* the saddest

[2] Country house of Frank Schuster.

season of the year if you do not take what is offered to you, and only yearn for the things that are far off: you should leave your flowers now & again, for a day, or two days be in London and go back refreshed & ready for flowers & good advice. I will enquire for the metronome—but In these days anything quiet is not counted & I have not seen a silent metronome for years.

The part-songs Op. 71, 72, 73 will not be ready yet—They are very big & you shall have them as soon as the printers send them. Do not work too hard at your choir—I am sending you some books on the training [?] of it. I have not seen the books but I hope they may have some practical ideas in them.

I am or have been better—last week I had another internal chill & am just recovering. Let me know when you come up—it will of course be soon now if even for the day or two days. Here all goes on as usual & I am worked very hard to little purpose having many many worries not worth writing about—but worth the telling—

With love
Yours sincerely
E. E.

A week later Elgar wrote again

Feb. 24th, 1914

Severn House
42 Netherall Gardens
Hampstead N.W.

Dear Rosa:

I am sending you via Novello a few of their primers which I hope will be useful—if they are not advanced enough let me hear (You may let me hear anyway!) and I will try to find something better suited to your requirement. I heard only today about the silent metronome. They are no longer made I am told—but a little *tape* indicator which I am sending may serve—I am sorry there is nothing of a better and more *present*-able quality.

The Birds are singing!
Yours sincerely,
E. E.

At this time of recollection of old days Elgar was in mind of taking up the oratorio trilogy, and memories of Longdon Marsh were awakened. Nostalgic moods were painful, and contained secret thoughts.

The enduring relationship between Edward and Rosa on the one hand, and between Rosa and Alice on the other, is a fact susceptible of various interpretations. To some extent each was dependent on the other in this triangular situation. Alice, one must remember, whatever her inner feelings, was the very embodiment of discipline—which meant self-discipline too. She had instructed her daughter as to the behaviour expected of a general's grand-daughter; from a general's daughter more was required.

During this period Alice looked back at some of her earlier writings. She expressed her regrets that she had not managed to write more, but she was "consoled by wise dictum—'the care of a genius is enough of a life work for any woman'". However, thinking on the death of her own youthful ambitions and the changes wrought by the years, she turned to one of her favourite pieces. *Two Summers*, and through the turn of events was soon convinced that it had a renewed value. The Elgars did not think in July that the summer of 1914 would be different from any other, and they went to Scotland for a holiday.

> Unsuspectingly on July 19th, we left London travelling by night to Glasgow, and then on by easy stages to Inverness. Our objective was Lairg, but on arrival we took an instantaneous dislike to the place and to the hotel in particular. We had booked for two weeks but somehow we managed to extricate ourselves and went on to Gairloch. This entailed a railway journey to Achnasheen and then a thirty mile drive to the Gairloch hotel. The taxi driver was slightly drunk and Father and I in the back of the car with our hearts in our mouths sang nonsense songs of which we had built up a good repertoire over the years; this at least distracted us and prevented our staring at the edges of deep precipices or watching with great uneasiness the edge of Loch Maree which came right up to the side of the road with no fence. Mother sat in front, quite happy and imperturbable; she never seemed to sense any danger in a car. We luckily arrived safely and found the hotel delightful. It had lovely grounds, sands quite near and lovely walks. Time passed all too quickly. But the news of the assassination of the Archduke was very disturbing and it was very difficult to get any news. Eventually we sent a telegram to Novello's to try and learn something of the situation. All our friends were on holiday and it was almost impossible to get in touch with anyone. It seems incredible that there was not even radio to tell us anything. War was declared, of course, on August 4th but we were unable to leave until the 10th as every available vehicle was commandeered to fetch the Territorials and the Lovat scouts from the entire district, and the little steamer was collecting men from the islands. It was very moving to watch

these men going off every day and all the way to London we were aware of the vast movement of men.

Once home, Father did not lose a minute in offering his services for the war contrary to what some people seem to believe that he went into the country and remained there for the remainder of the war. He went to Hampstead Police Station and was sworn in as a Special Constable. He also attended a meeting at which it was proposed to form an Artists' Corps. My Mother, full of indignation, embarrassed us by going into the local shops and asking how many recruits they had. Later, she found an outlet for her patriotism in teaching soldiers French and went to Chelsea Barracks for some weeks, until the C.O. stopped the lessons, much to her disappointment.[3]

Alice suffered further disappointment when her hopes of adding a much-needed inspirational note to the general exhortation were dashed by a brief, formal note from The Hepworth Manufacturing Co. Ltd., Cinematographers, of Walton-on-Thames:

> Messrs. Hepworth much regret after careful consideration that they are unable to accept the film entitled—"A Tale of Two Summers", and they beg to return the Scenario herewith.

To all outward view the Elgars were a supremely patriotic pair. Edward, however, found little about which to enthuse when civilisation appeared to be in total collapse. He simply did not know what was happening, least of all among the Germans whom he regarded so highly. He paid his dues to the public conscience and composed a number of works of greater or lesser relevance to the general situation. The great and significant works, however, were those which came after the war, the String Quartet, the Piano Quintet, and the Cello Concerto. All the while he languished in a state of spiritual discontent, from which his wife, his daughter, and his closest friends tried to rescue him.

Edward had spent a good deal of his life in the hands of medical practitioners, and it may be suspected that he always found the one who was least effective for his current complaint. In 1916 the family passed through a particularly worrying period. On 8 April—on his way to his sister's house in Worcestershire—Edward suddenly felt ill in the train. A Captain

[3] Carice Elgar Blake MS.

Dillon, in the same compartment, saw that something serious was amiss and removed Elgar at Oxford and saw to it that he was installed in the Acland Nursing Home. Alice meanwhile was suffering from influenza in Severn House. As soon as she had recovered she and Carice (now working in the Censorship Department of the War Office, in Kingsway) went to Oxford to learn that Edward had been the victim of an attack of Ménière's Disease. Certainly it scared him. To Rosa Burley, now known intimately as "Peggy" (derived from a popular musical, *Peg o' my heart*), he wrote:

Sunday April 30th 1916 Severn House
Hampstead N.W.

Dear Peggy,

I know how fine the gorse is and how everything is quivering with spring but I do not get on at all well & am very shaky indeed.

I am trying to get ready for the journey, which is long, but I should not be in the least surprised if it turned out to be the longest—a final joke of the poor old Arch-jester.

All good wishes
Yours sincerely,
E. E.

From time to time until Alice's death, Miss Burley came to visit at Severn House, and since she appeared able to lessen Edward's depressions Alice asserted satisfaction at such visits in her diary. She went along with her solemn duty to preserve the integrity of the genius she had married, or the genius whom through marriage she may have made.

But there was still a residual duty to herself. In a sense Alice's life had ended when she ceased to be Alice Roberts. With the departure from the scene of Alice Roberts, of Redmarley, there passed a personality more gifted than many, more industrious in respect of intellectual exercise than most, and genuinely creative. During a quarter-century of married respectability Alice Elgar emerged—a dedicated helpmeet (the saddest part of the story is her record of ruling bars on manuscript paper for Edward's convenience), a hostess who observed all the regulations concerning etiquette, a parent with rigid principles, and a contemner of all that seemed to be destructive of established values. But Alice still hankered after the old life.

One day she took aside Percy Anderson, designer of sets for D'Oyly Carte productions of Gilbert and Sullivan, and also for Elgar's *Crown of India*, read him *Isabel Trevithoe* and wondered whether that could be made into a play.

> I am afraid nothing ever came of the idea. Mother had great literary ambitions which she ruthlessly swept to one side when she married, but I know it gave her great pleasure if anyone was interested in her writings and she was intensely proud of the fact that Father had used her words, which he did several times.[4]

On 5 September 1914 Alice fell in, and reported for duty, writing a piece of terrifying banality addressed to the British common soldier. On 15 November Field-Marshal Lord Roberts died, and this recalled to Alice the long roll of her family's service in the nation's interests. Basing herself on the various traditions which she considered to be of especial worth she addressed herself to the nation through the medium of a sonnet.

England
August 4. 1914.

Holding her reign in kindly state and might,
Still deeming honour trod in knightly ways,
Half armed, lay England through the summer days;
Her rule, outspeeding dawn, outchecking night,
Welded the sphere in wide, majestic flight.
When lo! a foe appears who neither stays
Nor warns, but sweeps the Belgian plains and sways
Grim hosts and arrogates a devilish? *savage?* right.

[He said, 'Old] England sleeps *he said* and dreams of gain,
She will not stir, who once was battle's lord,
Or risk the clash of squadrons on the main;
Her treaties may be torn, while 'gainst the horde
These lesser folk may plead for help in vain.'
But 1914
Then, throned amidst the seas, She bared her sword.

R. A. Streatfeild, of the British Museum, a friend of these days, read through this poem and asked permission to submit it to the Editor of *The Bookman*. It was duly published in the August 1915 issue (No. 287, Vol. XLVIII), and given pride of place on the front page: The Editor introduced it thus:

[4] Carice Elgar Blake MS.

Lady Elgar, several of whose songs have been set to music by her husband, the famous composer, sends us the following lines, commemorative of England's entry into the World War.

Although Alice had the privilege of opening that issue (but propped up by her husband's fame) hers was not the most interesting contribution to a publication which otherwise included an essay on Samuel Butler by George Sampson, a Max Beerbohm cartoon of Bernard Shaw, a review of a new book on William Blake by Edward Thomas, and of H. G. Wells's *Bealby*.

Throughout 1915 Alice kept her patriotic fervour in full flood. When lost for occupation she wrote abusive phrases in her diary about Germans. After the sinking of the Lusitania she also felt strongly that it was high time the Americans recognised what their duty was. On 8 October she wrote a ruthless poem accusing them of being content merely to profiteer while their "kinsfolk" in Britain were left to defend the right.

Pay, pay, pay
Only pay enough and then
We glance aside, we Yankee men
And feasting, drown the accusing thought
That peace so meanly can be bought,
That murder flies on bloodstained wings,
And lays its claws on young and old and brings
A hellish torment to the earth.
But we, we revel in our mirth.

There followed four more stanzas of *Compensation* extending the general sentiment. Somewhere inside the placid Alice was hidden a good hater. Her last entry in her Diary for 1915 was

> End of year anxieties. D. G. much success in many ways to England. Sad losses and awful atrocities by the Germans who have become more diabolical than ever. May Victory for the Allies and peace come in the New Year.

Just at this moment Alice suffered a mishap. On 27 December —two days before the opening of *The Starlight Express*, which "E. wd. not conduct as the mise en scene was so repulsive—& was not even present"—she had an accident involving a taxi and was kept to the house for a month, during which Carice had special leave from the War Office to look after the household. It was shortly after that that Edward went down with Ménière's Disease.

In May 1917 the Elgars went into another country retreat, this time near Fittleworth, in Sussex. Alice and Carice, not sure whether their selection of country cottage would meet with Edward's approval, arranged an initial occupation of one month. But since Edward took to the place the tenancy was extended through the last years of Alice's life. All the time, however, it was Edward's health that was the prime concern. At the end of 1917 Alice wrote "Can only pray E. better soon and that a victorious peace may come".

In August the family had been in Hereford, and while Edward was in Manchester for a conducting engagement, she went back to Redmarley. Willie Baker drove her to her old house, where she saw how "the great oak had gone and the beloved ash perished". But the house was "charming" and Alice regretted that there had been so many things they would liked to have done but were never able to do:

1918

Father still seems to have been unwell early in the year and his Dr, Sir Maurice Abbott-Anderson, gave him tests of his nose and throat, and the test was satisfactory. In spite of this, he decided a few days later to have an X ray test; also negative and the whole condition was ascribed to a 'dropped stomach' for which electric treatment, and later a special belt, were recommended. It was a great relief to know that there was nothing radically or organically wrong. For the next few weeks he seems to have been very much up and down, after which he began to go for long walks; to the Cemetery at Highgate for instance, I happened to be free and to go with him, and we were completely staggered by its immensity and its astounding monuments. He went too to a lot of sale rooms and bookshops. Lady Stuart of Wortley, Algernon Blackwood, Sidney Colvin, Lalla van der Velde were frequent visitors, as also were the John Fortescues, who had just bought a lovely old house in Hampstead. This seems too to have been the beginning of friendship with the Bernard Shaws, as Lalla took Father to lunch with them. Also the first contact with Adrian Boult: 'Mr. Boult to tea, quite a nice quiet man'. Next day they went to his rehearsal at Queen's Hall where he was rehearsing. 'In the South'—'Too few strings, but reading of it really good'. If they could have foreseen !

Mr. Reed kept his promise of some months ago and brought

his Quartet to Severn House. Mother says they played beautifully but unfortunately she does not say what they played—but all their friends came to hear and she was very gratified to know that the Quartet enjoyed playing in the music room.

Father, though apparently better, was not really well and Sir Maurice, after consultation with Mr. Tilley, the throat surgeon of the day, strongly urged the removal of his tonsils and Father agreed. It worried Mother considerably that he should have such an operation at his age, 61, but he went into a nursing home in Dorset Square on March 14th and had the operation next day. All went well and the operation was fully justified as the tonsils proved more poisonous even than they had suspected. He was in a great deal of pain for several days; they were not anything like the sedatives etc that we have now, but nevertheless he woke up one morning and asked for pencil and paper and wrote down the opening theme of the 'Cello Concerto' and he was allowed home on March 22nd to Mother's great relief. He was disappointed at not feeling quite well straight away he began writing music and was working at the Quartet.

Mother was meanwhile very busy arranging for the move to Brinkwells for recuperation. She had to think what would be wanted in the country as there was a scarcity of furniture and comforts there and also the business of shutting up Severn House safely. Father's only contribution to all this was choosing tools which he would need for the woodwork he did and the repairs and small improvements he made. The great removal day was May 2nd and they went by train and were met by Mr. Aylwin with his pony cart and luggage cart and a warm welcome. I had joined them at Victoria and Father and I walked up. We had a warm welcome too from Mrs. Hewitt who 'did' for us.[5]

Next summer Alice was again put in memory of old time when Sarah Allen, now crippled with incurable neuritis, came to stay at Brinkwells.

The war over, the Elgars moved back into Severn House, and after remonstrating with local government officials about an inadequate fuel allowance (she pictured to the official England's greatest composer sitting cold and hungry while the country needed his services as never before) Alice learned of a translation project of Carice and went to the London Library to discover what Italian works would be the most use to her daughter. In the summer of 1919 Alice was glad once more to be able to refer a problem to her cousin Willie Raikes. While the Elgars

[5] Carice Elgar Blake MS.

were in Sussex the neighbours in Hampstead had cut down a row of trees between the two houses and were in process of building a garage below Edward's music room. Since there was no effective planning legislation to prevent such unneighbourly action there was not much that William Raikes could do.

In an effective sense Edward's career came to an end in 1919, with the first performance of the String Quartet and the Piano Quintet in May, and of the Cello Concerto in the autumn. The preparations for the latter were fairly disastrous. The work was included in a London Symphony Orchestra programme otherwise to be conducted by Albert Coates, who was less than sensitive to Elgar's susceptibilities. So it was that the composer was kept waiting for an hour before he could begin to rehearse on 26 October. Alice was beside herself with rage: "An insult to E. from that brutal, selfish ill mannered bounder A. Coates". Next day Coates was equally unaccommodating. The performance, however, went off tolerably well—though the size of the audience reflected a certain coolness towards the "new" Elgar. But the following day passions were still running high. Alice expressed herself thus: "Still furious about rehearsals—*shameful.* Hope never to speak to that brutal Coates again".

Alice's life had been fraught with anxieties, and she was temperamentally ill adapted to accepting change. She had, of course, had to accommodate herself to numerous changes, of lifestyle, of residence, of status, and of belief. But, rooted in the patterns of the past and with a determination to restore herself to what she had come from, while taking her husband with her, she could not face the brave new world of 1920. So she gradually took herself away from it.

What Alice wrote about Albert Coates was less a commentary on him than on the disruptions which occurred in the wake of the war. On 26 September 1919 the railwaymen went on strike. Next day—when in fact, the strike was called off—Alice wrote: "Traitors, they ought to be shot—worse than the worst enemies —& they have no excuse". In November she took to her room, feeling "rather badly", and, under medical supervision, she spent most of the rest of that year there. She characterised the year as "in many ways as regards disturbances, strikes, trials, finance, a serious one—Fear not much joy in it for E. except in writing his wonderful music".

With the New Year came a determination to resume the normal round. Alice went visiting, she occasionally lunched out, she went to some plays and some concerts. But by March she was patently seriously ill. Afflictions of kidneys and heart, and the inadequacies of medical treatment, led to rapid decline. She died on the morning of 7 April 1920. Later that day A. H. Fox Strangways came to Severn House where "at my Father's special request"[6] he wrote the obituary that appeared in *The Times* of 8 April. The headline "Devoted Helpmeet of Master Musician" set the tone for every other obituary. Edward received telegrams of commiseration from the King and the Queen, from Queen Alexandra, and from Princess Louise, Duchess of Argyll. The funeral took place at St. Wulstan's, Little Malvern, on 10 April.

A month later Mrs. Caroline Dighton, daughter of Rev. Robert Raikes, Vicar of Longhope, and Alice's aunt, died at Newland in the Forest of Dean, in her ninety-eighth year. In 1921 Aunt Gertrude, the once fearsome Lady Thompson, died in Sussex. Next year Alice's surviving brother, Napier, died in Cheltenham. On 1 June 1923, Arabella Veronica Raikes, the widow of Stanley Napier Raikes, who had been celebrated as an invalid fifty years before, died in her ninety-seventh year and on 6 June her body was taken back to Dymock for burial in the pretty churchyard that lies across the valley from, and in sight of, Hill Ash. Among those of the family waiting at the Green, outside the church, was Sir Edward Elgar. At the end then he was accepted on his own merits as a member of society to which Alice had belonged.

With the death of "Aunt Vee" the complex tale of the intertwined dynastics of Probyn, Raikes, Dighton, Roberts, came to an end. And the end of the story was the music of Elgar.

The marriage between Edward Elgar and Alice Roberts was one which survived, because each partner depended on the other for protection against isolation. When they arrived at the point of marriage they were in one way detached from their antecedents by ambition and imagination, but they were

[6] Carice Elgar Blake MS.

bound by loyalty to the landscape and traditions of their region. By marriage Alice largely cut away her own ambitions—to be a writer—and substituted for them those of Edward. It was, as she conceived it, her duty. In the course of time under the pressure of duty Alice became merely boring, both on the subject of Edward's music, and in herself. Edward knew this, and sought emancipation from the tedium of constricted domesticity by sharing his thoughts with friends. Of these friends, some made as many claims on him as he on them. This is particularly true of the women friends who flit across the pages of history, and in respect of whom Alice was singularly indulgent.

Her life's reward was to be a Lady, with which title she managed to maintain family dignity. But, as she had intended, she had made a great composer. It was not the fact that she ruled the scoring paper for Edward that mattered, but that when he first needed encouragement she knew the right kind of encouragement to be administered and where it was to be found. Before his marriage Edward as a composer was unknown. After his marriage he was introduced to those among his wife's acquaintances who could extend his connections among the regionally influential. However unpalatable it may now seem, to be the husband of the daughter of a Major-General was at one time a factor not to be ignored.

It was remarked sometimes how Sir Edward Elgar affected a military bearing. This—a total contradiction to the least military of men—was an unconscious offering for Alice, whose philosophy had derived from the code obeyed by her father and mother. Alice herself was so obedient to the code that she destroyed her own personality. The Victorian daughter became the Edwardian mother, and the story of Alice Roberts–Elgar is a sad one. At the beginning there was an eager girl exploring a world filled with wonder. At the end a prematurely old woman, soured by the actuality of the social changes which once indeed she had foreseen. She ended her life not in Marchcroft Manor—but in Severn House, and a long way from home.

Epilogue

A poem written by Edward Elgar while living at "Forli"
The Tired Soul

With the closing of the eyes
Wearied thought to heaven-ward flies
Grows more ample, — unrestrained, —
Reaching to the unattained:
Earthly littleness forgot,
Petty strifes concern us not,
Free the mind and soul uprise
With the closing of the eyes

Anxious loved ones, — hand in hand
Rise with us to the land
Where, o'er golden floors, untrod
Fields of dew and shining mist.
Streams a wider, deeper flow
Of Harmony than earth may know;
Sounds too deep for us unwise
~~With the~~ closing of the eyes.
Come with!

x x x x x

Dreams, you say: — alas! that we
Should
Must ever quit that shining sea
For petty ~~strifes~~ cares and small distress,
Earth and all its littleness.

Surely, as the time now flies *
Breaking dearest links & ties: *
One day we shall gather ~~up~~ close;
We may gather all our loves
Our loves

With the longed-for last sweet sleep
And closing of the weary eyes.

Edward Elgar

Appendix I

POETRY AND PROSE WORKS OF CAROLINE ALICE ELGAR

Poems unless otherwise stated.

1873 (?) *Worlds from my Window /a/ Geological Essay*, 58–60

1876 20–23 October *The Portrait* (short story), 70–71, 100, 114

1877 3 June, *The Flower and the Star; A Fantasy:*
11 November *Family Pride*
n.d. *Marian's Party*
n.d. *Human Life: A Simile*
n.d. *Down, down, down, Down to the depths of the sea*[1]
n.d. *The Snowflake*[2]
} stories for children, 62

27 December *Autumn*, 63
28 December *The Reply*[3], 63
29 December *The Snow* (For a Child)[4], 63, 74

1878 February *Thought*
25 April *Senlac*, 63
30 June *Then he leapt upon his Horse*[5]
3 July *The Fight for the Shrine*[6], 63, 155
14 August *Miserrimus: Inscription on a Tomb in Worcester Cathedral*, 63, 64
27 August *On a Castle in N. Ireland*[7], 64
6 November *To ——* , 64
She answers
22 December *New Year*
n.d. [*Four*] *Songs of the Seasons and Hope*[8], 64
n.d. *I know a Pretty Bell*[9]

1879 14 April *Isabel Trevithoe: A Poem by C.A.R.*[10], 12, 70, 71–5, 100, 117
14 April *Désillusionné*, 64
14 April *Telle est la vie . . . quelquefois*, 64
11 November *To the Sea at Porth-kernow* [Porth-curnow][11], 64
n.d. *On the Wings of the Wind: A Night Journey to the Arctic*: story for children[12], 68–9

1880 1 June *The Golden Stair—suggested by the picture of Burne-Jones*[13], 65
[1880] 21 June *Yesterday*[14], 66
July *Storm or Calm*[15], 66–7
15 August *The Wind at Dawn*[16]
13 September *Full long ago in Arcadie*
1882 6 April To G.E.L. [ander?]. *Born on All Hallow E'en*, 83
July *Marchcroft Manor: A Novel in Two Volumes*, published Remington Ltd., 12, 38, 40–41, 61, 70, 75–9, 81, 100, 114, 145
n.d. *He would be a Hero:* children's story, 68
1883 n.d. *Whither?*, at Bordighera, 83
1884 17 May *Two Summers*[17], 79–80, 174
1886 18 March *A Ballad of 1886*, 84–5
1887 25 March *Lyre and Song*[18], 87–8
31 March *To emulate Marcus Aurelius*, 88, 155
25 July *An Admonition against Despondency*, 86
October *Renunciation*, 90, 155
9 October *Sonnet: Ways to the Mount*, 91, 155
19 November *A Benison*, 91
1888 30 January *Sonnet: "The Friend of the Bridegroom . . . rejoiceth greatly"*, 92, 155
11 February *O Happy Eyes*[19], 92
March *"It is appointed to all men to die once"*[20], 93
29 April *The World it is wide*
8 May *On hearing some orchestral music*[21], 94
1 June *A Courtyard in Granada (A Courtyard is seen beyond)—suggested by a picture of the above name in the Grosvenor Gallery*, 155
16 August *Love's Grace*, 94, 155
26 December *Most dear my own belovèd, let us hold*, 96–7
n.d. *Statue in the Italian Exhibition*[22]
1889 December(?) *The Sunny Isles*[23], 103, 155
13 December *The Night is still*[24], 104
Flies the Frost
1890 20 April *Fair breaks the Spring*[25], 107
1892 25 August *A Spear, A Sword*, 112
26 August *1588: Loose, loose the Sails*[26], 112, 155
6 December *The Millwheel* I "Winter", 113, 155
II "May (a Rhapsody)", 113–14, 155
1894 January *Above the Clouds*[27]
4 January *The Wave*
Muleteer's Song[28]
1895 *Words for six Bavarian partsongs for Chorus and Orches-*

tra/Music by Edward Elgar. To E.E. from C.A.E. 5 March 1895, 115–35
(1) "The Dance (Zum [*sic*] Zugspitze/Im Sonnenbiche)"
(2) "Aspiration (Wamberg)"
(3) "Lullaby (Bei Hammersbach)"
(4) "False Love (Bei Sanct Anton)"
(5) "The Marksman (On the Alm)"
(6) "True Love"[29]
(7) "Nought broke the Summer Silence (On the Kitzbühler [Horn][30]
n.d. *Ritter Gluck*, trs. from Uhland[31]
21 June *After*
October *Sighs in Summer*[32], 143, 155
1897 May *Love alone*[33], 143
1898 17 November *The Dying* [*Warriors*] *Heroes*, trs. from L. Uhland, 155
1900 20 July (?) *The Violin*, trs. from the Italian
1901 *Love in Absence*, 144
19 February *Reconciliation: Come back, the sea lies still*, 144–5
1904 16 November *Something afar*
1907 6 December *A Christmas Greeting*[34], 161–3
1909 25–27 December *The Kingsway*[35], 165
1914 20 November *4 August 1914*[36], 177
1915 5 September–8 October *Compensation*[37], 178

Undated pieces
Three Sonnets:
Longing in Absence
Longing again
Love would give itself
Two Sonnets—*Links*
We strive, we labour, holding our own race
And if mere links we are, why yet despair?
Sonnet translated from the Vita Nuova (Dante):
So tender and so holy seems to be, 155
Twilight—a set of ten sonnets
Two lives
Long had I wandered weary through the world
rewritten as *A Vision of the Night*
Flies the frost & sighs the wind—"December 21st"
Something afar "words free", 155
Calypso's Lament, note by Elgar, "Begin lines where marked"
On the way, 155
Atalanta's Race

Destiny
Self-Delusion
Love's answers (Elvira to Bevis)
Love and Death (After seeing Mr. Watts' Picture)[88], 155
Twelve Sonnets
New Year
Mr. Hamilton's Grave
The world's wide space will know my name[89]
Deep of earth's joys they drink[40]

Prose
The Ideal in the Present, 145 ff.
Impressive things seen & heard
Things seen

Poems by Edward Elgar
After a week's house hunting (1890), 105–6
Drafts to show rhythmic patterns for *Songs of the Bavarian Highlands,* 118 ff.
The tired Soul, 184–5

NOTES

1 Prefaced by quotation from Keats
2 Prefaced by quotation from Tennyson
3 Author's note: "I trust a happier faith now. C.A.E. (1890)"
4 Author's note: "9 a.m."
5 Author's note: "In Mem. 5 May '78"
6 Title *Apollo Belvedere* deleted; see Sidney Colvin, "The Apollo Belvedere", *New Quarterly Magazine* X, April–October 1878, pp. 31–46
7 Author's note: "from V[era]'s description of a Castle on the north coast of Ireland".
8 Recopied, with author's note: "For E.E. from C.A.E.", and on No. 2 "A.W.B. wopse"
9 On Hazeldine writing-paper
10 Published by Charing Cross Publishing Company 1879, but presentation copy from author to F. B. Roberts dated 27 November 1878. *The Snow* and *Fly singing Bird,* set as partsongs by Elgar in 1894 (Op. 26, nos. 1 & 2), were interludes in *Isabel Trevithoe*
11 See Roden Noel, "Rambles by Cornish Seas", *Macmillan's Magazine* XXXIV, 1876, pp. 334–41
12 Described as "by the author of *Isabel Trevithoe*"
13 *The Golden Stairs,* by E. C. Burne-Jones, exhibited in Grosvenor Gallery, May 1880

14 Published in *Home Chimes,* 2 August 1884
15 Revised from earlier version author's note: "A true picture of A's self", July 1880; revised August or September 1888
16 *Home Chimes,* 16 August 1884; set by Elgar, 1888
17 Published in *Home Chimes,* 17 May 1884
18 Author's note: "D'Oyly Walk"
19 Set by Elgar for S.A.T.B., Op. 18 No. 1 (Novello 1896)
20 Suggested by a sermon by W. J. Knox Little, 4 March
21 Alternative title: *On hearing a certain Piece of Music.* Reference to performance of Elgar's *Three Pieces for String Orchestra,* Worcestershire Musical Union, 7 May 1888
22 Author's note: "Eros clinging to a maiden's shoulder & covering her eyes with his hands" [Item 193 in the Catalogue of *The Italian Exhibition* in London 1888 was "Love & Desire"]
23 One draft marked "An Imitation"; to replace original text of *My Love dwells in a Northern Land* (A. Lang)
24 Author's note: "For New Year to E.E."
25 Author's note: "For Mrs. W. A. Raikes"
26 Diary entry for this day: "Miss Simpson sang his songs".
27 Pencil note by C.E.B. "Probably after a walk in the hills above the clouds, Dec. 31 1893—see Diary"
28 Diary entry, 4 January: "The Wave/Muleteer's Song/From Froissart [Rondel WAR]"
29 The texts of Elgar's *From the Bavarian Highlands,* Op. 27, in nos. 1–6
30 Pencil sketch
31 Published in *London Society, a Monthly Magazine,* May issue
32 Elgar's: "If you smells, this, zu'll find its not fesh grhh! E."
33 Diary, 30 May 1897: "E. wrote out Song—"Love Alone" Miss Burley brought back Carice & sang it": published in *The Dome* (1898): see *Sea Pictures,* Op. 37 (II "In Haven (Capri)")
34 Author's note: "Rome"; set by Elgar for 2 S., 2 vl., pfte., ded. to G. R. Sinclair and his choir for their Carol Concert 1907.
35 Set by Elgar as a solo song, perf. Alexandra Palace, London, 15 January 1910; Diary entries: 24 January, "E. thinking of song for March Trio"; 25 January, "E. arranging to words "The King's Way" for song March Trio tune; 27 January, "Orchestrating 'The King's Way' "
36 or *Autumn 1914: England,* published in *The Bookman, No.* 287 Vol. XLVIII, August 1915
37 Original title *Pay, pay, pay*
38 This picture (1874) existed in various versions. That now in the Manchester Art Gallery was exhibited in Birmingham in 1886
39 On "Forli" writing-paper
40 On "Severn House" writing paper.

Appendix II

Fragments towards opera libretti. These may date from 1909, for in May of that year, while the Elgars were in Italy, the idea of composing an opera was under discussion. This idea had been stimulated by a Mr. Welch, from the U.S.A., who one day arrived on the Elgars in Florence with a libretto of his own compilation. That Elgar began seriously to consider writing an opera at that time is indicated by a sketch book labelled, "Opera in three Acts—Edward Elgar—Careggi—May, 1909". It is, then, tempting to read the first of the two fragments below into this situation. The last line of the second links up with the ultimate *The Spanish Lady*, which also incorporates London crowd scenes.

I

Mita & girls [pick] gathering herbs—dispersed around—Then girls come up with arms full & throw all in a great heap—with joyful gestures at work being done, now they can dance—begin—Mita does not join them—declines & wanders pensively around—suddenly hears a step crackling amongst the trees, looks up expectantly & Giorgione appears—they greet each other happily then with great spirit join the dance. At the height of dance more footsteps are heard 2 servitors are seen leading richly caparisoned mule riderless, & bearing a litter made of branches on wh. lies apparently helpless & almost lifeless, an old man in rich dress—The dancers start back then gather round as the litter stops seeing the little crowd—

II

Sc. I *Coast of Barberry*

An excited crowd rushing to the sea shore, stormy, a raging sea is dashing a distressed ship on the rocks—Some of the shipwrecked men reach the land with the help of fragments of wood &c—Seized by the native & pitilessly dragged off [.] Captives—One of them Gilbert à Beckett distinguished by his height & lofty presence is looked on as a special prize.

Sc. II *Royal Castle at Capital*

Old King & his daughter Noora & guests—Princes, Visitors—King points out alterations to his prince Visitors, they are amazed at fresh splendours—he tells them they were brought about by a northern captive. He is ushered in, very noble looking, with a stern sad countenance—He, Gilbert & Noora exchange glances & as the company move about the Hall exchange words.

Sc. III

Suddenly trumpets sound, a messenger is announced, the ransom for Gilbert has arrived. Great sensation—Noora faints.

Sc. IV Later

Same Hall. Solemn assembly, King exhorts Gilbert to stay—has given his word that he may go if ransomed—Gilbert asks for Noora's hand—King furiously refuses, threatens him with death if he does not leave the country next morning—

Gilbert received message through Noora's attendant that he must say farewell to her—[Just] Before dawn all still darkness one of her devoted slaves leads him by devious unknown ways to her apartments midst all sorts of difficulties & dangers—Passionate farewell & Gilbert promises to try some means of returning & carrying her off—He goes & starts for England.

Act II Some months later

Gilbert in his home in London—Considerable splendour—He is talking with his friend Harold who with others asks why does he look so sadly taking no interest in hawk nor hound, in war or peace—or making gold. Gilbert evades their questionings, G. & H. [friends] show much affection for one another—Harold & the rest leave. [Harold goes out says he has to seek a friend down at the river's edge & leaves.] Gilbert bemoans his fate, he cannot set off to Barberry & is broken hearted. His father is dying he cannot leave him—*Il mio padre si muove, non posso lasciar lo —che fare? Dio mio pietà per me, per* Noora—goes out—

Sc. 2

[Harold &] [By the river—] [A ship just in from the East.] [Crowd rough—confusion—Amongst those] The friends leaving G. walk together one of them, Eustace tells H. a strange tale that a girl who looks as if she came from the far East has been seen walking thro' the streets saying only one word, as if calling someone—over & over again, Harold laughs [?] & says it cannot be true. Eustace says it is & wishes he cd. see her—the friends part—Harold walks on alone—Presently hears voices, sees a little crowd, & there is the girl, some ruffians are annoying & trying to seize her, he rushes up, draws his sword & scatters them. The girl is nearly fainting & clings to him in gratitude, Harold overcome with her beauty [.] The girl can only sob & utters no word—Harold leads her off to his house [.] Gives her in the care of his old nurse—Has fallen deeply in love—

When rested & restored next day Harold visits her in the nurse's company, shows much gratitude but only says a word something like Gilbert,—Harold connects it in no way with his friend—for sometime —This goes on [—] Harold loves her—She is proud & distant—He shows her his fine house & signs that he lays it all at her feet—She haughtily repulses all. Meanwhile Gilbert has heard of the wandering girl & is mad with wonder & roams round unceasingly [*sic*] seeking in case it might be some one Noora might have sent never dreaming Noora cd. have escaped. Tells no one & becomes worn & thin. At last he pours his sorrows out to Harold & tells him all—Harold at once sees it must be Noora & is astonished [—] the word Gilbert never made him suspect anythg. He is inwardly heartbroken but conceals it. Invites G. to a great banquet [.] Says he is to be married & G. must be chief guest. G. has to consent [.] Time comes & G. finds himself at head of table a vacant place by him—Harold goes out, music blazes & Harold returns leading in Noora, rapture &c—

All sorts of incidents illustrate London life—apprentices &c.

Bibliography

The Geological Magazine, London 1864–73
The New Quarterly Magazine, London 1878, Vol. X
The Grosvenor Gallery—Illustrated Catalogue of the Summer Exhibition, with Facsimiles of Sketches by the Artists, ed. Henry Blackburn, London 1878–90
Robert Raikes et ses Ecoliers, H. Laune: a free translation of *Robert Raikes and his Scholars* (London 1880), Paris 1881
Littlebury's Guide to Worcester, Worcester 1883
Chambers's Journal, London 1883
Pictorial Malvern, Malvern [1885]
Rev. Edward V. Hall, Precentor of Worcester Cathedral, Formerly Incumbent of Trinity Church, Brighton, *Sermons Preached in Worcester Cathedral*, London 1887
W. J. Knox Little, *Sunlight and Shadow in the Christian Life*, London 1889 (dedicated to Rev. Morgan Dix, Rector of Trinity Church, New York)
Pocket Diary for the Malverns, Malvern 1899–1901
The Malvern ABC, Malvern 1891–2
City of Gloucester: Interesting Features—Industrial, Natural, Archaeological, Residential, Gloucester Traders' Association [1898]
L. Huxley, *Life and Letters of Sir J. D. Hooker*, London 1918, 2 vols.
F. O. Bower, *Joseph Dalton Hooker*, London 1919
T. Bainbrigge Fletcher, *Cotteswold Naturalists' Field Club: 1846–1946*, Gloucester 1946
B. Turrill, *Joseph Dalton Hooker*, London 1963 (with a picture of Sir Joseph and Lady Hooker in late life)

Index

View in Dean Forest, near Ruardean.
Pencil drawing by Sir William Guise, Bart.,
for *Records of the Rocks.*